Edexcel A2 Music Listening Tests scores booklet

Question 2: Aural Awareness (2015)

Test 1 (2015)

Test 2 (2015)

Blank page

Test 3 (2015)

Kommt ein schlank - er Bursch ge - gan - gen, blond von_ Lo - cken o - der braun,

hell von__

ei, nach_ dem kann man wohl schau'n, ei, nach_ dem kann man wohl schau'n, ei, nach

dem, nach_ dem kann man wohl schau'n! Zwar schlägt man das_

Aug' auf's Mie - der nach ver - schäm - ter_ Mäd - chen Art; doch ver - stoh - len hebt man's

wie - der, wenn's das Herr - chen nicht ge - wahrt, doch_ ver - stoh - len hebt_ man's

Test 4 (2015)

Question 2: Aural Awareness (2016)

Test 1 (2016)

Test 2 (2016)

den Him - mel an.   Fleuch,

(a) notate melody

Nach - ti - gall, in grü-ne Fin - ster nis - se, ins Hain - ge-sträuch,   und

(b) (ii) cadence B   *cadence C*

ent - fleuch!

Test 3 (2016)

Blank page

Test 4 (2016)

Question 2: Aural Awareness (2017)

Test 1 (2017)

Test 2 (2017)

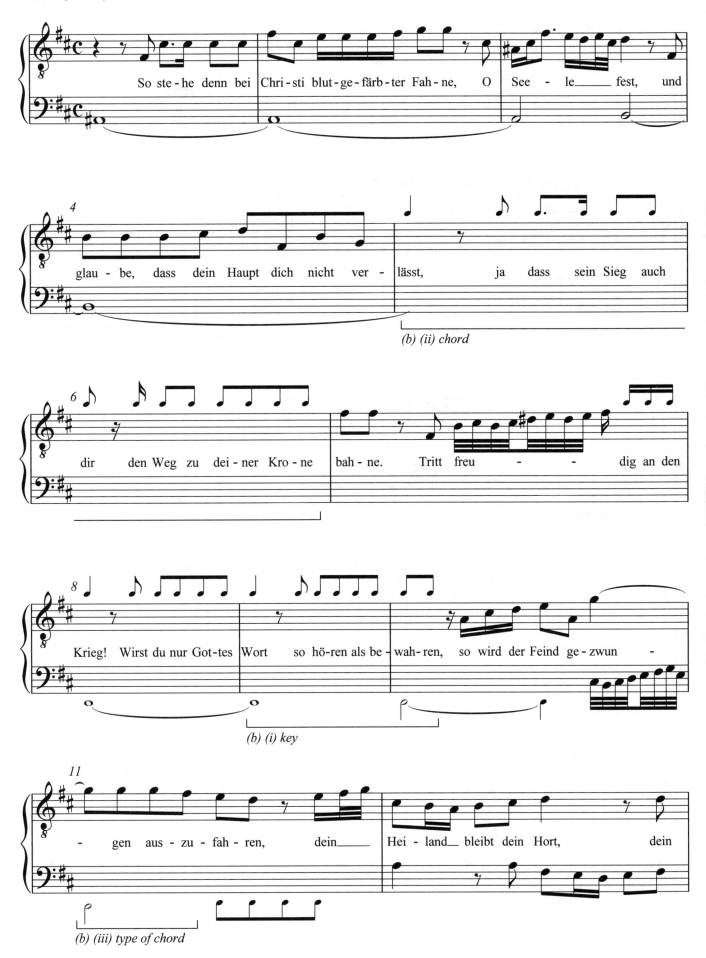

So ste - he denn bei Chri - sti blut - ge - färb - ter Fah - ne, O See - le ____ fest, und

glau - be, dass dein Haupt dich nicht ver - lässt, ja dass sein Sieg auch

(b) (ii) chord

dir den Weg zu dei - ner Kro - ne bah - ne. Tritt freu - - dig an den

Krieg! Wirst du nur Got - tes Wort so hö - ren als be - wah - ren, so wird der Feind ge - zwun -

(b) (i) key

- gen aus - zu - fah - ren, dein ____ Hei - land ____ bleibt dein Hort, dein

(b) (iii) type of chord

Hei - land___ bleibt dein Hort, dein Hei - land ___ bleibt___ dein___ Hort._____

_____ dein Hei-land bleibt dein Hort.

(b) (iv) cadence

(b) (v) dissonance

(b) (i) key

Translation:

So stand by Christ's blood-spattered banner, my soul, and trust in his everlasting protection.
Yes, he will help you gain your crown of victory.
Go forth joyously to the fight!
If you hear God's word, and do as he commands, no foe will prevail against you,
your salvation will be sure and your refuge secure.
Blessed is he who praises God.

Test 3 (2017)

Test 4 (2012)

2015–2017

A2 Music
Listening Tests

Edexcel

Hugh Benham

and

Alistair Wightman

RHINEGOLD
EDUCATION

www.rhinegoldeducation.co.uk

Music Study Guides

GCSE, AS and A2 Music Study Guides (AQA, Edexcel and OCR)
GCSE, AS and A2 Music Listening Tests (AQA, Edexcel and OCR)
GCSE, AS and A2 Music Revision Guides (AQA, Edexcel and OCR)
AS/A2 Music Technology Study Guide (Edexcel)
AS/A2 Music Technology Listening Tests (Edexcel)
AS and A2 Music Technology Revision Guides (Edexcel)

Also available from Rhinegold Education

AS and A2 Music Harmony Workbooks
GCSE and AS Music Composition Workbooks
GCSE and AS Music Literacy Workbooks
Musicals in Focus, Romanticism in Focus, Baroque Music in Focus, Film Music in Focus, Modernism in Focus
Music Technology from Scratch
Careers in Music
Dictionary of Music in Sound

First published 2014 in Great Britain by
Rhinegold Education
14–15 Berners Street
London W1T 3LJ, UK
www.rhinegoldeducation.co.uk

© 2014 Rhinegold Education,
a division of Music Sales Limited

You should always check the current requirements of the examination, since these may change. Copies of the Edexcel specification can be downloaded from the Edexcel website at www.edexcel.com.
Edexcel Publications telephone: 0845 1720205, email: publication.orders@edexcel.com

Edexcel A2 Music Listening Tests
Order No. RHG352
ISBN: 978-1-78305-583-8

Exclusive Distributors:
Music Sales Ltd
Distribution Centre, Newmarket Road
Bury St Edmunds, Suffolk IP33 3YB, UK

Printed in the EU

Contents

The authors

Hugh Benham read Music and English at Southampton University, where he was awarded a PhD for his study of the music of John Taverner. He is a chair of examiners for GCE Music, an in-service trainer, church organist and writer, and formerly taught music in a sixth-form college. Hugh has contributed to *Music Teacher* and *Classroom Music* magazines, and is the author of *Baroque Music in Focus* (Rhinegold Education, 2nd ed. 2010). His other writing includes two books on English church music, including *John Taverner: his Life and Music* (Ashgate, 2003), articles on early music, contributions to *The New Grove Dictionary of Music and Musicians* (2001) and *Die Musik in Geschichte und Gegenwart*, and a complete edition of Taverner for *Early English Church Music*.

Alistair Wightman read Music at Oxford and then York University, where he was awarded a D.Phil for his study of the music of Karol Szymanowski. He has worked in primary, secondary and further education, and is a freelance teacher and writer as well as principal examiner in history and analysis for A level music. His publications include *Writing about Music* (Rhinegold Education, 2008) and several books and articles devoted to Tadeusz Baird, Karlowicz and Szymanowski, including *Karlowicz, Young Poland and the Musical Fin-de-siècle* (Ashgate, 1996), *Karol Szymanowski: his Life and Music* (Ashgate, 1999) and *Szymanowski on Music: Selected Writings of Karol Szymanowski* (Toccata Press, 1999).

Acknowledgements

The authors would like to thank the consultant Paul Terry and the Rhinegold Education editorial and design team of Harriet Power and Ben Smith for their expert support in the preparation of this book.

Audio tracks

A CD containing recordings of all the extracts for the listening tests in this book is available to buy separately from Rhinegold Education (978-1-78305-584-5, RHG353).

The publisher and authors are grateful to all those who have given permission to use their recordings.

Introduction

What this book is for

This book is to help you to do as well as you possibly can in the Further Musical Understanding exam for Edexcel A2 Music (Unit 6). Here you will find various listening tests for Section A of the Unit 6 exam, and also advice and specimen questions to help you prepare for Sections B and C.

How to use this book

➤ **If you are taking the exam in 2015**, first use the listening tests labelled '2015' in Section A (pages 9–12 and 28–31). The listening tests labelled '2016' and '2017' will however provide you with additional valuable practice. In Sections B and C, read the general advice and then concentrate on the questions labelled '2015' (pages 41–42).
➤ **If you are taking the exam in 2016**, first use the listening tests labelled '2016' in Section A (pages 13–16 and 32–36). The listening tests labelled '2015' and '2017' will however provide you with additional valuable practice. In Sections B and C, read the general advice and then concentrate on the questions labelled '2016' (pages 41–42).
➤ **If you are taking the exam in 2017**, first use the listening tests labelled '2017' in Section A (pages 17–20 and 37–40). The listening tests labelled '2015' and '2016' will however provide you with additional valuable practice. In Sections B and C, read the general advice and then concentrate on the questions labelled '2017' (pages 41–42).

For the listening tests in Section A, this book contains spaces in which to write your answers, and for the Aural Awareness questions we have provided the necessary skeleton scores. The music that you must listen to in order to answer the Section A questions can be found on the accompanying CD (RHG353), which can be bought separately from Rhinegold Education.

When working through the exercises, you might want to keep to exam conditions as closely as possible, for example by listening to the music for each test the regulation number of times, observing the appropriate lengths of pauses and so on (there's more on this on pages 7–8). But, early on in the course especially, you can use the tests as practice and learning material rather than as pretend exam questions – for example, by listening to excerpts more times than possible in the exam. Try working through some tests a second time once you have had a chance to forget the answers.

Examination requirements

You must read the full examination requirements as set out in the specification (or syllabus) for Edexcel A2 Music. Your teacher will have a copy, but the information can also be accessed from the Edexcel website (www.edexcel.com). **Remember that specifications can change *and* that some requirements are specific to particular years.** It is your teacher's responsibility and yours to know all about the relevant examination requirements.

Examiners' top tips

Apart from as much listening experience as you have time for, and plenty of practice at each type of test, examiners recommend the following:

1. **Learn the correct technical words.** You must know these because they sometimes appear in the questions and should be used in your answers.

Some sources of information on technical words are given on page 7, in the introduction to Section A.

2. **Read each question thoroughly** and do exactly what it requires. Correct and relevant information gets marks; irrelevant information does not (even if it is true).

3. **Believe your ears!** In listening tests, write about what you actually hear, rather than what you expect to hear.

4. **Note how many marks are available for each question.** For example, if there is a bracketed three (3) after part of a question, this means that three marks are available, and that you will generally need to make three points in your answer.

5. **Avoid getting bogged down,** especially on questions that carry only a single mark. Near the end of your exam, you may have time to return (refreshed) to answers originally left incomplete.

6. **Manage your time carefully.** You have two hours for the Unit 6 exam. Section A is structured for you – you listen to a CD with all the music you need and there are pauses between the excerpts for you to write your answers. For Sections B and C together you will probably have just under an hour and a half. As Section B carries 26 marks, and Section C 36 marks, it is sensible to spend longer on the latter than on the former. There's no hard-and-fast rule, but you might spend 35–40 minutes on the two 13-mark questions that make up Section B, and the remainder of your time (probably some 50–55 minutes) on the extended essay in Section C.

Section A: Aural Analysis

There are two questions – entitled 'Comparison' and 'Aural Awareness' – which are worth 10 and 18 marks respectively (together they make up 28 of the 90 marks for the whole Unit 6 paper).

Comparison question

For comparison questions, you have to identify and comment on musical features from two excerpts, comparing and contrasting them as required. In the exam you will hear each excerpt three times, in the order A, B; A, B; A, B. There will not be a break between A and B, but there will be a pause after each hearing of Excerpt B. The first two pauses will be 30 seconds in length, and the third (during which you complete your answers) will last for 2 minutes.

In comparison questions, be ready to think about the following musical features:

➤ Melody
➤ Rhythm and metre
➤ Harmony
➤ Tonality
➤ Texture
➤ Form (structure)
➤ Instrumental and/or vocal forces.

> Remember especially that 'tonality' usually means 'key' in Unit 6 – not tone quality or anything like that. 'Harmony' refers to individual chords and successions of chords, and is not an alternative term for accompaniment. For further brief comments on these features, see the glossary (page 72) and recent examiners' reports for Edexcel A2 Music. See also the *Dictionary of Music in Sound* (Rhinegold Education, 2002).

In each comparison question, you will be asked to place the excerpts in their historical, social or cultural context (notably by identifying genres, composers and dates of composition). The excerpts will be taken from a piece (or from two different pieces) that may be unfamiliar to you. The music chosen will, however, be related in some way to one or more of the set works that you study for Section B and/or Section C.

Although this leaves a vast number of possibilities, it does help to suggest a structure for the listening part of the course. If there is a set work by Bach or Stravinsky, for example, you might listen to other music by the composer in question. If you are studying a trio sonata or fugue, it is a good idea to hear other trio sonatas (and similar chamber-music genres) or other fugues.

The more music you hear, the better equipped you will be to name genres, composers and dates. In fact, the only way to do this is to compare what you are trying to identify with what you have previously heard. Listening to music that you don't know and may not like isn't easy – little and (very) often is a good maxim. There's always the chance, if you listen widely and are open-minded, that from time to time you will come across something unexpectedly wonderful!

Aural awareness question

What we have just said applies equally to the aural awareness question, because again you will be asked to comment on the music's context.

In addition, you will be asked in each test to recognise chords and keys, and complete a dictation task (that is, to write down in musical notation something you have just heard played or sung). You will have to listen to only one excerpt of music, which in the exam you will hear five times, with the following pauses: 30 seconds after the first hearing, 1 minute after the second, 1 minute after the third, 30 seconds after the fourth, and 3 minutes after the fifth. To help you with the aural awareness question, there is a single- or two-stave skeleton score of the music.

Aural dictation may come easily to you or you may need a lot of practice, depending partly on how familiar you are with staff notation. It is a skill worth persevering with, apart from anything to do with the exam: for example, it can be very useful to write down musical ideas when there is a risk of forgetting them and when no means of making a recording is available.

Start by working through the dictation examples on pages 21–27. It is easier to begin with these separate, short examples than with the tests that are embedded in longer pieces of music. Ask your teacher to make up some more if you run out altogether. Why not also try writing your own tests for your friends to do?

To be able to recognise chords and keys is useful in many forms of music-making, including composing and improvising. You may need a lot of practice with it: one good plan is to work or rework the activities in chapter 2 of the AS *Music Harmony Workbook* (Rhinegold Education, 2008).

Question 1: Comparison (2015)

Test 1   **Tracks 1–2**

The following questions require you to compare and contrast two excerpts of music (which we will call A and B) from the same work. Listen to both excerpts three times in the order A, B; A, B; A, B.

As explained on page 7, Excerpt B should follow Excerpt A without a break each time. There should be a 30-second pause after the first and second hearings of Excerpt B. Allow yourself 2 minutes after the third hearing of Excerpt B in order to complete your answers.

(a)   Contrast the use of string instruments in the two excerpts.

....

....

....   **(3)**

> The question tells you that both excerpts have strings – so you need to comment on some different ways in which the strings are deployed, in particular referring to any solo instruments.

(b)   Name the type of longer work from which these excerpts come.

....   **(1)**

> Your response to (a) above may help you answer (b).

(c)   How do the two excerpts differ in texture?

....

....   **(2)**

(d)   Indicate whether the statements below are true or false by placing a cross in the appropriate box.

    (i)   Only Excerpt A is in compound time.   TRUE ☒   FALSE ☒

    (ii)   Descending chromatic melodic lines
        appear in both excerpts.   TRUE ☒   FALSE ☒   **(2)**

(e)   Put a cross in the box next to the name of the composer of these excerpts.

   ☒ **A** Corelli   ☒ **B** Gabrieli   ☒ **C** Monteverdi   ☒ **D** Vivaldi   **(1)**

(f)   Suggest a possible year of composition.

....   **(1)**

(Total 10 marks)

Test 2   **Tracks 3–4**

The following questions require you to compare and contrast two excerpts of music from the same work. Listen to each excerpt three times in the order A, B; A, B; A, B; with pauses as indicated on page 9.

(a) Put a cross in the box next to the **one** statement below which is true.

☒ **A** Both excerpts begin in a major key

☒ **B** Both excerpts begin in a minor key

☒ **C** Excerpt A begins in a major key; Excerpt B begins in a minor key

☒ **D** Excerpt A begins in a minor key; Excerpt B begins in a major key   **(1)**

(b) Identify **two** differences between the vocal melodic lines of the two excerpts.

1. ....

2. .... **(2)**

(c) Comment on the tempi of the two excerpts.

....

.... **(2)**

> 'Tempi' is plural of 'tempo' (musical speed or pace).

(d) Name **two** types of chord used only in Excerpt B, which make its harmony more tense than the harmony of Excerpt A.

1. ....

2. .... **(2)**

(e) Name the type of longer work from which Excerpts A and B are taken.

.... **(1)**

(f) Put a cross in the box next to the year in which these excerpts were composed.

☒ **A** 1735   ☒ **B** 1770   ☒ **C** 1805   ☒ **D** 1840 **(1)**

> You will get a mark for a correct answer to (f) even if, later on, you contradict it when answering question (g). Try though, as far as possible, to think about questions on years and composers together, so that the answer to one helps you with the answer to the other.

(g) Put a cross in the box next to the name of the composer of these excerpts.

☒ **A** Beethoven   ☒ **B** Handel   ☒ **C** Mozart   ☒ **D** Wagner   **(1)**

(Total 10 marks)

Test 3   **Tracks 5–6**

The following questions require you to compare and contrast two excerpts of music from the same work. You will hear each excerpt three times in the order A, B; A, B; A, B; with pauses as indicated on page 9.

(a) Much of Excerpt A is based on a motif with three different pitches, the first two of which are B and C. What is the third pitch?

....   **(1)**

(b) Describe **one** way in which the composer treats this motif.

.... **(1)**

(c) Comment on the melodic writing in the first (slow) section of Excerpt B.

....

.... **(2)**

The question asks for comment on 'melodic writing' (e.g. on stepwise or leaping movement, or how motifs are used), not for identification of instruments. You will have the chance to comment on instrumentation in part (e).

(d) What wind instrument, accompanied by strings, plays a solo in the second part of Excerpt A (after the staccato rising scales)?

....   **(1)**

(e) Describe the instrumentation and texture of the first (slow) section of Excerpt B.

....

....

.... **(3)**

(f) Suggest a possible composer of these excerpts.

....   **(1)**

(g) Put a cross in the box next to the year in which these excerpts were composed.

☒ **A** 1910   ☒ **B** 1940   ☒ **C** 1970   ☒ **D** 2000   **(1)**

(Total 10 marks)

Test 4

The following questions require you to compare and contrast two excerpts of music in the same musical style. You will hear each excerpt three times in the order A, B; A, B; A, B; with pauses as indicated on page 9.

(a) Name **two** rhythmic features common to both excerpts and typical of the style.

   1. ....

   2. .... **(2)**

(b) In which excerpt do several melodic phrases end with a descending, stepwise motif of three notes?

   .... **(1)**

(c) Comment on the instrumentation and textures in the introductions to these excerpts.

   ....

   ....

   ....

   .... **(4)**

(d) Name the solo instrument heard at the end of Excerpt B.

   .... **(1)**

(e) Put a cross in the box next to the style that best describes these excerpts.

   ☒ **A** Bebop   ☒ **B** Traditional jazz   ☒ **C** Ragtime   ☒ **D** Twelve-bar blues   **(1)**

(f) Put a cross in the box next to the year in which these excerpts were recorded.

   ☒ **A** 1912   ☒ **B** 1927   ☒ **C** 1942   ☒ **D** 1957   **(1)**

(Total 10 marks)

Question 1: Comparison (2016)

Test 1   **Tracks 9–10**

The following questions require you to compare and contrast two excerpts of music (which we will call A and B) from the same work. Listen to both excerpts three times in the order A, B; A, B; A, B.

As explained on page 7, Excerpt B should follow Excerpt A without a break each time. There should be a 30-second pause after the first and second hearings of Excerpt B. Allow yourself 2 minutes after the third hearing of Excerpt B in order to complete your answers.

(a) What vocal resources are used in Excerpt A?

....

.... **(2)**

(b) Compare and contrast the vocal resources used in Excerpt B with those used in Excerpt A.

....

.... **(2)**

> The expression 'vocal resources' in parts (a) and (b) refers to the types of voices (not instruments) used, and to the use of soloists and/or choir.

(c) Name the wind instrument that has a solo part in Excerpt A.

....   **(1)**

> Solo instrumental parts in Baroque music are often called 'obbligato' (note spelling with double 'b'), to stress that they are vital to the musical texture, and therefore obligatory.

(d) How do the excerpts differ in texture?

....

.... **(2)**

(e) Name the type of longer work from which these excerpts are taken.

....   **(1)**

(f) Suggest a possible composer for these excerpts.

....   **(1)**

(g) Put a cross in the box next to the year in which these excerpts were composed.

   ☒ **A** 1686   ☒ **B** 1726   ☒ **C** 1766   ☒ **D** 1806   **(1)**

(Total 10 marks)

Test 2   **Tracks 11–12**

The following questions require you to compare and contrast two excerpts of music from different works by the same composer. You will hear each excerpt three times in the order A, B; A, B; A, B; with pauses as indicated on page 13.

Both excerpts are in fast triple metre.

(a)   Describe the texture and instrumentation of the opening four-bar phrase of Excerpt A.

Texture ....

Instrumentation .... **(2)**

(b)   In terms of texture and instrumentation, how is the opening four-bar phrase of Excerpt B:

    (i)   **Similar** in texture to the opening phrase of Excerpt A?

    ....

    (ii)   **Different** in instrumentation from the opening phrase of Excerpt A?

    .... **(2)**

(c)   What type of woodwind instrument is heard **only** in Excerpt B?

    .... **(1)**

(d)   Indicate **two** ways in which the tonality of Excerpt B differs from that of Excerpt A.

    1.   ....

    2.   .... **(2)**

> Questions on tonality do not expect you to identify aurally the actual keys used (e.g. F major or B minor).
> They just expect references to use of major or minor, and/or to change(s) of key.

(e)   Excerpt A is from a Minuet. From what type of movement, also in triple time, is Excerpt B?

    .... **(1)**

(f)   Name the type of multi-movement work from which both excerpts come.

    .... **(1)**

(g)   Put a cross in the box next to the name of the composer of these excerpts.

    ☒   **A** Brahms   ☒   **B** Haydn   ☒   **C** Schubert   ☒   **D** Tchaikovsky   **(1)**

(Total 10 marks)

Test 3   **Tracks 13–14**

The following questions require you to compare and contrast two excerpts of music from the same work. You will hear each excerpt three times in the order A, B; A, B; A, B; with pauses as indicated on page 13.

(a)   Contrast the melodic writing in the opening vocal phrases of each excerpt.

....

.... **(2)**

> Concentrating on a single phrase from each excerpt may seem difficult, but each phrase is heard more than once (to different words), which should help.

(b)   Contrast the handling of rhythm and metre in each excerpt.

....

....

.... **(3)**

> When you listen without a score, it can be impossible to identify the time signature exactly (in particular, to tell the difference between $\frac{2}{4}$ and $\frac{4}{4}$, or $\frac{2}{4}$ and $\frac{2}{2}$). If you write $\frac{2}{4}$ and the score says $\frac{4}{4}$, you won't be marked wrong, but more general observations are preferable, such as 'duple or quadruple metre'.

(c)   Comment on the tonality of each excerpt.

Excerpt A ....

Excerpt B .... **(2)**

(d)   Name the type of longer work from which these excerpts are taken.

.... **(1)**

(e)   Put a cross in the box next to the year in which these excerpts were composed.

☒ **A** 1917   ☒ **B** 1937   ☒ **C** 1957   ☒ **D** 1977   **(1)**

(f)   Put a cross in the box next to the name of the composer of these excerpts.

☒ **A** Bernstein   ☒ **B** Gershwin   ☒ **C** Cole Porter   ☒ **D** Lloyd Webber **(1)**

(Total 10 marks)

Test 4   **Tracks 15–16**

The following questions require you to compare and contrast two excerpts of music from different works by the same composer. You will hear each excerpt three times in the order A, B; A, B; A, B; with pauses as indicated on page 13.

(a)   Put a cross in the box next to the term describing the type of scale widely used in the melodic material of both excerpts.

   ☒ **A** Minor   ☒ **B** Modal   ☒ **C** Pentatonic   ☒ **D** Whole-tone   **(1)**

(b)   Compare and contrast the harmony of the two excerpts.

   ....

   ....

   ....   **(3)**

(c)   Describe the textures of Excerpt A.

   ....

   ....

   ....   **(2)**

(d)   Using a single word, describe the texture at the beginning of Excerpt B.

   ....   **(1)**

(e)   What type of non-European music influenced the composer in these excerpts?

   ....   **(1)**

(f)   Put a cross in the box next to the decade in which these excerpts were composed.

   ☒ **A** 1870s   ☒ **B** 1900s   ☒ **C** 1930s   ☒ **D** 1960s   **(1)**

(g)   Suggest a possible composer for these excerpts.

   ....   **(1)**

(Total 10 marks)

Question 1: Comparison (2017)

Test 1   **Tracks 17–18**

The following questions require you to compare and contrast two excerpts of music (which we will call A and B) from the same work. Listen to both excerpts three times in the order A, B; A, B; A, B.

As explained on page 7, Excerpt B should follow Excerpt A without a break each time. There should be a 30-second pause after the first and second hearings of Excerpt B. Allow yourself 2 minutes after the third hearing of Excerpt B in order to complete your answers.

(a)   Name a percussion instrument heard in Excerpt B but not in Excerpt A.

      ....   **(1)**

(b)   Contrast the tempo and rhythm of the two excerpts.

      ....

      ....   **(2)**

(c)   Name the instrument playing the melody in the second half of Excerpt B.

      ....   **(1)**

(d)   How do the melodies of the excerpts differ?

      ....

      ....

      ....   **(3)**

(e)   Name the type of multi-movement orchestral work from which these excerpts are taken.

      ....   **(1)**

(f)   Put a cross in the box next to the composer of these excerpts.

      ☒ **A** Cage   ☒ **B** Pheloung   ☒ **C** Shostakovich   ☒ **D** Stravinsky   **(1)**

(g)   Suggest a possible year of composition.

      ....   **(1)**

                                                                          (Total 10 marks)

Test 2   **Tracks 19–20**

The following questions require you to compare and contrast two excerpts of music (which we will call A and B) from the same work. Listen to both excerpts three times in the order A, B; A, B; A, B.

(a)   Name two instruments heard in Excerpt A but not in Excerpt B.

    1.   ....

    2.   ....   **(2)**

(b)   Give three similarities between the excerpts.

    1.   ....

    2.   ....

    3.   ....   **(3)**

(c)   Apart from the texts set, give three differences between the excerpts.

    1.   ....

    2.   ....

    3.   ....   **(3)**

(d)   In which of the following time spans were the excerpts composed?

    ☒ **A** 1550–1580   ☒ **B** 1600–1630   ☒ **C** 1650–1680   ☒ **D** 1700–1730   **(1)**

(e)   Put a cross in the box next to the composer of these excerpts.

    ☒ **A** Bach   ☒ **B** Corelli   ☒ **C** Monteverdi   ☒ **D** Sweelinck   **(1)**

(Total 10 marks)

Test 3   **Tracks 21–22**

The following questions require you to compare and contrast two excerpts of music (which we will call A and B) from the same work. Listen to both excerpts three times in the order A, B; A, B; A, B.

(a)   Contrast the use of voices in these excerpts.

....

....

....   **(3)**

(b)   (i)   Name a prominent solo instrument heard shortly after the start of Excerpt A.

....   **(1)**

(ii)   Name a percussion instrument heard in Excerpt B but not Excerpt A.

....   **(1)**

(c)   Indicate whether the statements below are true or false by placing a cross in the appropriate box.

(i)   Ostinato is used in Excerpt A.   TRUE ☒   FALSE ☒

(ii)   Dotted rhythms are used only in Excerpt B.   TRUE ☒   FALSE ☒

(iii)   The Dorian mode is used in both excerpts.   TRUE ☒   FALSE ☒   **(3)**

(d)   Put a cross in the box next to the composer of these excerpts.

☒ **A** Bernstein   ☒ **B** Britten   ☒ **C** Shostakovich   ☒ **D** Walton   **(1)**

(e)   Suggest a possible year of composition.

....   **(1)**

                                                                                                (Total 10 marks)

Test 4   **Tracks 23–24**

The following questions require you to compare and contrast two excerpts of music (which we will call A and B) from different works by the same composer. Listen to both excerpts three times in the order A, B; A, B; A, B.

(a) Name two instruments heard in Excerpt B but not Excerpt A.

    1.   ....

    2.   ....   **(2)**

(b) What effect for strings is used only in Excerpt B?

    ....   **(1)**

(c) Compare and contrast the textures of the two excerpts.

    ....

    ....

    ....   **(3)**

(d) Contrast the rhythm and metre of these excerpts.

    ....

    ....   **(2)**

(e) Put a cross in the box next to the composer of these excerpts.

    ☒ **A** Berlioz   ☒ **B** Handel   ☒ **C** Mozart   ☒ **D** Schubert   **(1)**

(f) Put a cross in the box next to the year when this music was composed.

    ☒ **A** 1744   ☒ **B** 1784   ☒ **C** 1824   ☒ **D** 1864   **(1)**

(Total 10 marks)

Dictation exercises

The exercises that follow are to help in the early stages of practice by isolating the dictation task from other aspects of Question 2 (Aural Awareness). Nevertheless, to begin getting used to hearing dictation in context, the exercises have a little given material before and after the part(s) you have to complete.

> In a few cases, tests have been very slightly adapted from the original pieces of music, which are identified in the answers section on pages 50–53.

To ease you into the process of dictation, in tests 1–5 we have asked you to supply note values in some places and pitches elsewhere, not both at the same time. Where pitches have to be supplied, the note values are shown; where note values are to be added, the pitches are given.

> Before tackling tests 1–5 you should have worked with more straightforward and shorter examples. Even supplying just one or two missing note values or one or two pitches can be valuable in the very early stages. Try 'self-dictation': hear a melody in your head, or sing it aloud, and try writing it down.

In each of tests 6–21, as in the exam, a passage is left entirely blank, for you to supply both note values and pitches. You are free to experiment and discover what method of working suits you best, but it may help to start with note values and then add pitches (or to work the other way round), rather than try to supply both melody and rhythm at once. The first time you hear a test, it can help just to decide how many notes there are – perhaps by putting a dot over the stave for each note you hear. You might then want to go straight to using conventional notation, but if it helps, start by indicating pitch with letter names (e.g. A, B, C♯, D), or rhythm by using a grid to show where each note comes in relation to the beat or pulse.

> Most tests use the treble clef, like Edexcel's sample question, and as appears likely in future assessments. The bass-clef tests are a reminder that these are not actually excluded by the specification. For additional bass-clef practice, ask someone to play other tests one or two octaves lower, taking care to avoid too many leger lines.

Practicalities

Your teacher, or someone else, can play a test from the answers section on pages 50–53, while you have in front of you the actual test with blank bar(s) from pages 22–27. Tests can be played on the piano or any other suitable instrument. A tempo mark is suggested, but in early practice the music can be played more slowly if necessary. The person playing the test can begin by sounding the tonic chord of the key in which the test starts, but bear in mind that this will not happen in the exam – you must identify the key from the context.

If there is no one at hand to play the tests for you, go to the relevant book page at www.rhinegoldeducation. co.uk. After you have registered on the site you will be able to access some MP3 files and download them to your computer or iPod. Tests 1–3 and 5 have been recorded twice – the first time considerably slower than the second.

Alternatively, you may be able to access the music for some tests on CDs or from iTunes. This would enable you to hear the underlying harmony, as happens in the exam, but there can be difficulties with this method, such as locating the precise bars you have to work with.

It does not matter in the early stages how many times you hear a test, but as you approach the exam, limit the number of playings to five.

To monitor your progress, each time you do a test, count up the number of pitches and/or the number of note values you get correct, and turn these into a percentage. Regard 40% or more of the total as good progress, and 70% or more as very encouraging.

Where a solution indicates that there are, for example, nine notes to be supplied, you need to reckon on *nine note values and nine pitches.* A 'note' is a single sound: occasionally a 'note' may have to be written as two symbols tied together.

Examiners' top dictation tips

➢ Identify the key at the beginning of each piece of dictation. Does it change as the test goes on?

➢ Some tests require you to add pitches that carry accidentals. Such accidentals are vital – if you miss them out, the notes that should have had them are counted as wrong.

➢ Sometimes a pattern that you need to add can be worked out from one of the given passages. Be alert to the possibility of straight repetition or melodic sequence.

Test 1

Supply the missing note values in bars 2 and 6–7.

Test 2

Supply the missing pitches in bars 2 and 5–6.

Test 3

Supply the missing note values in bars 3–4, and the missing pitches in bars 7–8.

Test 4

Supply the missing note values in bars 3–4, and the missing pitches in bars 6–7.

Test 5

Supply the missing pitches in bars 5–6, and the missing note values in bar 8.

Test 6

Supply the missing notes from bar 5 (last quaver beat) to bar 8 (third quaver beat).

Test 7

Supply the missing notes from bar 2 (fourth quaver beat) to the end of bar 3, and the pitch of the final note (bar 4).

Test 8

Supply the missing notes from bar 2 (second crotchet beat) to the end of bar 3.

Test 9

Supply the missing notes from bar 2 (fourth quaver beat) to the end of bar 6.

Test 10

Supply the missing notes from bar 2 (second crotchet beat) to bar 3 (first half of fourth crotchet beat).

Test 11

Supply the missing notes from bar 4 (fourth crotchet beat) to bar 7 (first crotchet beat).

Test 12

Supply the missing notes in bars 3 and 4.

The passage you have to complete includes (like bar 1 and bars 5–7) some triplet quavers.

Test 13

Supply the missing notes in bars 4–7.

Test 14

Supply the missing notes from bar 1 (fourth crotchet beat) to bar 3 (second crotchet beat).

Test 15

Supply the missing notes from bar 2 to the start of the third crotchet beat in bar 4.

Test 16

Supply the missing notes from bar 5 (third quaver beat) to the end of bar 7.

Note the large interval at the start – a major 6th. The passage features two other 6ths – one major and one minor.

Non troppo vivace

Test 17

Supply the missing notes from bar 3 (fourth crotchet beat) to bar 5 (first crotchet beat).

Andante

Test 18

Supply the missing notes from bar 1 (last quaver beat) to bar 3 (second crotchet beat).

[Andante]

Test 19

Supply the missing notes in bars 3–4.

Hint: this melody is pentatonic (apart from the short D♭s in bars 1 and 5).

Cantabile

Test 20

Supply the missing notes from bar 3 to bar 7 (second quaver beat).

Andantino sostenuto (ma non troppo)

Test 21

Supply the missing notes from bar 5 (last crotchet beat) to bar 7.

Here's something a little lighter and easier to finish with!

Cheerfully

Question 2: Aural Awareness (2015)

Test 1   **Track 25**

You will hear an excerpt of music five times. The playings will be separated by pauses.

➤ After the first playing, there should be a 30-second pause
➤ After the second playing, there should be a 1-minute pause
➤ After the third playing, there should be a 1-minute pause
➤ After the fourth playing, there should be a 30-second pause
➤ After the fifth and final playing, allow yourself 3 minutes to complete your answers.

There is a skeleton score on pages 2–3 of the score insert, which you must follow as you listen to the music for this test.

(a) Write out the missing melody line in bars 30–32. You may work in rough on the skeleton score, but you must copy your answer onto the stave below.

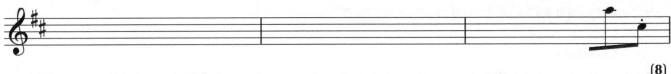

                                                                                  (8)

(b) (i) Identify the **two** chords in bar 8, first and second crotchet beats.

    Chord A ....

    Chord B ....   **(2)**

   (ii) Identify the key and cadence in bars 11–12 and 21–23.

    Bars 11–12 ....

    Bars 21–23 ....   **(4)**

   (iii) Identify the type of chord used in bar 18, second crotchet beat.

    ....   **(1)**

> The expression 'type of chord' means that you don't have to give a roman numeral, as in (b) (i). For a 'type of chord' question, the answer instead might be something along the lines of 'augmented sixth', 'diminished seventh' or 'Neapolitan sixth'.

(c) (i) From what type of multi-movement work is this excerpt taken?

    ....   **(1)**

   (ii) Put a cross in the box next to the name of the composer of this music.

    ☒ **A** Bach   ☒ **B** Beethoven   ☒ **C** Brahms   ☒ **D** Haydn   **(1)**

   (iii) Suggest a possible year of composition for this work.

    ....   **(1)**

                                                                      (Total 18 marks)

Test 2   **Track 26**

You will hear an excerpt of music five times. The playings will be separated by pauses as indicated on page 28.

There is a skeleton score on page 4 of the score insert, which you must follow as you listen to the music for this test.

(a) Complete the melody line in bars 26–28. You may work in rough on the skeleton score, but you must copy your answer onto the stave below.

(8)

(b) (i) Name the type of dissonance used in the following places:

Bar 6, first dotted-crotchet beat ....

Bar 14, first quaver beat   .... (2)

> The expression 'type of dissonance' covers passing notes, auxiliary notes, suspensions, appoggiaturas, etc.

(ii) Identify the **three** chords indicated in bars 9 to 11.

Chord A (bars 9–10) ....

Chord B (bar 11, first dotted-crotchet beat)   ....

Chord C (bar 11, second dotted-crotchet beat) .... (3)

(iii) Name the key to which the music modulates in bars 25–26.

.... (1)

(iv) Identify the cadence in bars 31–32.

.... (1)

(c) (i) Name the type of work from which this excerpt is taken.

.... (1)

(ii) Put a cross in the box next to the name of the composer of this music.

☒ **A** Bach   ☒ **B** Beethoven   ☒ **C** Mendelssohn   ☒ **D** Mozart   (1)

(iii) Put a cross in the box next to the year when this music was composed.

☒ **A** 1756   ☒ **B** 1786   ☒ **C** 1816   ☒ **D** 1846   (1)

(Total 18 marks)

Test 3   **Track 27**

You will hear an excerpt of music five times. The playings will be separated by pauses as indicated on page 28.

There is a skeleton score on pages 6–7 of the score insert, which you must follow as you listen to the music for this test.

(a)   Write out the melody line of bars 14–16. You may work in rough on the skeleton score, but you must copy your answer onto the stave below.

(8)

(b)   (i)   Identify the type of chord used in bars 25 and 26.

        Chord A (whole of bar 25) ....

        Chord B (whole of bar 26) ....   **(2)**

    (ii)   Identify the key of the music at bar 27.

        ....   **(1)**

    (iii)   Identify the cadence and key in bars 43–44, and in bars 54–55.

        Bars 43–44 ....

        Bars 54–55 ....   **(4)**

(c)   (i)   From what type of extended work is this excerpt taken?

        ....   **(1)**

    (ii)   Put a cross in the box next to the name of the composer of this music.

        ☒ **A** Bach   ☒ **B** Haydn   ☒ **C** Mozart   ☒ **D** Weber   **(1)**

    (iii)   Put a cross in the box next to the year when this music was first performed.

        ☒ **A** 1731   ☒ **B** 1761   ☒ **C** 1791   ☒ **D** 1821   **(1)**

(Total 18 marks)

Test 4   **Track 28**

You will hear an excerpt of music five times. The playings will be separated by pauses as indicated on page 28.

There is a skeleton score on pages 8–9 of the score insert, which you must follow as you listen to the music for this test.

(a) Write out the melody line of bar 21 (third crotchet beat) to bar 23 (first crotchet beat). You may work in rough on the skeleton score, but you must copy your answer onto the stave below.

> Think carefully about the first note. (Clue: it has an accidental, and is a note heard a little earlier in the piece.) The start of a dictation question is vital, because if you get the first note wrong it may be difficult to capture some of what follows. Sometimes, however, you can work backwards from the first note in the skeleton score that follows the gap you have to fill.

(8)

(b) (i) Identify the key at the marked passages in:

Bars 8–9   ....

Bars 12–13 .... (2)

(ii) Identify the type of chord used in each of the following locations:

Bar 8, second minim beat   ....

Bar 11, third crotchet beat .... (2)

(iii) Explain the relationship between the marked passage in bars 17–19 and the preceding passage (bracketed in bars 14–16).

.... (1)

(iv) Identify the cadence in bar 24.

.... (1)

(v) Identify the **two** chords in bar 26.

Chord A ....

Chord B .... (2)

(c) (i) From what type of work is the excerpt taken?

.... (1)

(ii) Put a cross in the box next to the name of the composer of this music.

  ☒ **A** Corelli   ☒ **B** Handel   ☒ **C** Purcell   ☒ **D** Vivaldi   (1)

(Total 18 marks)

Question 2: Aural Awareness (2016)

Test 1   **Track 29**

You will hear an excerpt of music five times. The playings will be separated by pauses.

➤ After the first playing, there should be a 30-second pause
➤ After the second playing, there should be a 1-minute pause
➤ After the third playing, there should be a 1-minute pause
➤ After the fourth playing, there should be a 30-second pause
➤ After the fifth and final playing, allow yourself 3 minutes to complete your answers.

There is a skeleton score on pages 10–11 of the score insert, which you must follow as you listen to the music for this test.

(a) Write out the melody line of bars 24–25. You may work in rough on the skeleton score, but you must copy your answer onto the stave below.

                                                                                                    (8)

(b) (i) Name the type of dissonance that is heard three times in the lower part in bars 9–11.

        ....   (1)

> 'Types' of dissonance include anticipations, appoggiaturas, auxiliary notes, passing notes and suspensions.
> For information on types of dissonance, see the glossary, page 72.

   (ii) Identify the **two** chords in bar 36.

        Chord A ....

        Chord B ....   (2)

   (iii) Name the key in bars 41–44, and the type of cadence.

        Key   ....

        Cadence ....   (2)

   (iv) Identify the key through which the music passes:

        In bars 46 to 48 (first crotchet beat) ....

        In bar 62 ....   (2)

   (v) Identify the key at the end of the excerpt.

        ....   (1)

(c) (i) Of what type of piece is this music the beginning?

        ....   (1)

(ii) Put a cross in the box next to the name of the composer of this music and the approximate date of composition.

☒ **A** J. S. Bach, 1730   ☒ **B** Mozart, 1790

☒ **C** Mendelssohn, 1830   ☒ **D** Brahms, 1890   (1)

(Total 18 marks)

Test 2   **Track 30**

You will hear an excerpt of music five times. The playings will be separated by pauses as indicated on page 32.

There is a skeleton score on pages 12–13 of the score insert, which you must follow as you listen to the music for this test.

> Brahms' song was originally in the key of E major. The skeleton score here is in D major, which matches the recommended recording.

(a) Complete the melody line of bars 49–53. You may work in rough on the skeleton score, but you must copy your answer onto the stave below.

(8)

> Although the melody line you have to add extends for more than four bars, there are no more than twelve notes to write. Clue: melodic sequence is used. Write down the first note of bars 49, 50 and 51 to give a kind of framework, before adding in the remainder of bars 49 and 50.

(b) (i)   Identify the chord heard in bar 3. ....   (1)

    (ii)   Identify each of the following cadences:

        Cadence A (bars 6–7)   ....

        Cadence B (bars 54–55)   ....

        Cadence C (bars 55–57) ....   (3)

    (iii) Identify the key in:

        Bars 10–14 ....

        Bars 25–27 ....   (2)

    (iv)   Precisely identify the harmonic device employed in bars 13–20.

        ....   (1)

    (v)   Identify the chord heard in bar 34, first minim beat. It is in the tonic minor key, D minor.

        ....   (1)

(c) (i)   Put a cross in the box next to the type of song heard in this test.

        ☒ **A** Aria   ☒ **B** Ballad   ☒ **C** Lied   ☒ **D** Mélodie   (1)

    (ii)   Suggest a possible composer for this song. ....   (1)

(Total 18 marks)

Test 3   **Track 31**

You will hear an excerpt of music five times. The playings will be separated by pauses as indicated on page 32.

There is a skeleton score on page 14 of the score insert, which you must follow as you listen to the music for this test.

(a) Write out the missing melody line in bar 14. You may work in rough on the skeleton score, but you must copy your answer onto the stave below.

(8)

(b) (i) Identify the key and cadence in bars 4 and 18.

Bar 4: Key   ....

Cadence ....

Bar 18: Key   ....

Cadence ....   (4)

(ii) Identify the chord or type of chord used at each place indicated in bar 7.

Chord A ....

Chord B ....

Chord C ....   (3)

(c) (i) Put a cross in the box next to the type of longer work from which this excerpt is taken.

☒ **A** Anthem   ☒ **B** Mass   ☒ **C** Opera   ☒ **D** Passion   (1)

(ii) Put a cross in the box next to the name of the composer of this music.

☒ **A** Bach   ☒ **B** Handel   ☒ **C** Haydn   ☒ **D** Purcell   (1)

(iii) Put a cross in the box next to the year when this music was first performed.

☒ **A** 1667   ☒ **B** 1697   ☒ **C** 1727   ☒ **D** 1757   (1)

(Total 18 marks)

Test 4   **Track 32**

You will hear an excerpt of music five times. The playings will be separated by pauses as indicated on page 32.

There is a skeleton score on pages 16–17 of the score insert, which you must follow as you listen to the music for this test.

(a)   Write out the melody line of bars 6–9. You may work in rough on the skeleton score, but you must copy your answer onto the stave below.

(8)

For additional practice, after you have completed questions (a)–(c), try adding the missing melody line of bars 36–38.

(b)   (i)   Identify the chords indicated in bars 13–16.

Chord A ....

Chord B ....   (2)

(ii)   Identify the key of bars 22–26, and the cadence.

Key   ....

Cadence ....   (2)

(iii) Name the type of chord heard at the end of bar 39.

....   (1)

(iv) Identify the key through which the music passes in bars 47–49.

....   (1)

(v)   Identify precisely the harmonic device used in bars 53–60.

....   (1)

(c)   (i)   What contrapuntal device is used in the opening bars of this excerpt?

....   (1)

(ii)   Suggest a year of composition for this music.

....   (1)

(iii) Put a cross in the box next to the name of the composer of this music.

☒ A Bach   ☒ B Beethoven   ☒ C Berlioz   ☒ D Brahms   (1)

(Total 18 marks)

Question 2: Aural Awareness (2017)

Test 1   **Track 33**

You will hear an excerpt of music five times. The playings will be separated by pauses.

➤   After the first playing, there should be a 30-second pause
➤   After the second playing, there should be a 1-minute pause
➤   After the third playing, there should be a 1-minute pause
➤   After the fourth playing, there should be a 30-second pause
➤   After the fifth and final playing, allow yourself 3 minutes to complete your answers.

There is a skeleton score on page 18 of the score insert, which you must follow as you listen to the music for this test.

(a)   Complete the melody line of bars 54–56. You may work in rough on the skeleton score, but you must copy your answer onto the stave below.

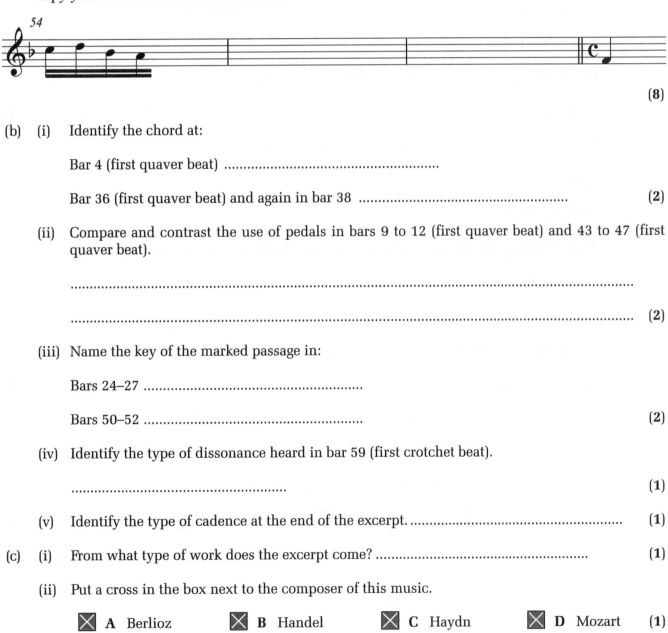

                                                                                                                                                        (8)

(b)   (i)   Identify the chord at:

           Bar 4 (first quaver beat) ....

           Bar 36 (first quaver beat) and again in bar 38 ....   **(2)**

      (ii) Compare and contrast the use of pedals in bars 9 to 12 (first quaver beat) and 43 to 47 (first quaver beat).

           ....

           ....   **(2)**

      (iii) Name the key of the marked passage in:

           Bars 24–27 ....

           Bars 50–52 ....   **(2)**

      (iv) Identify the type of dissonance heard in bar 59 (first crotchet beat).

           ....   **(1)**

      (v)   Identify the type of cadence at the end of the excerpt. ....   **(1)**

(c)   (i)   From what type of work does the excerpt come? ....   **(1)**

      (ii) Put a cross in the box next to the composer of this music.

           ☒ **A** Berlioz   ☒ **B** Handel   ☒ **C** Haydn   ☒ **D** Mozart   **(1)**

                                                                                                                                    (Total 18 marks)

Test 2   **Track 34**

You will hear an excerpt of music five times. The playings will be separated by pauses as indicated on page 37.

There is a skeleton score on pages 19–21 of the score insert, which you must follow as you listen to the music for this test.

(a)   Complete the melody line of bars 41–43. You may work in rough on the skeleton score, but you must copy your answer onto the stave below.

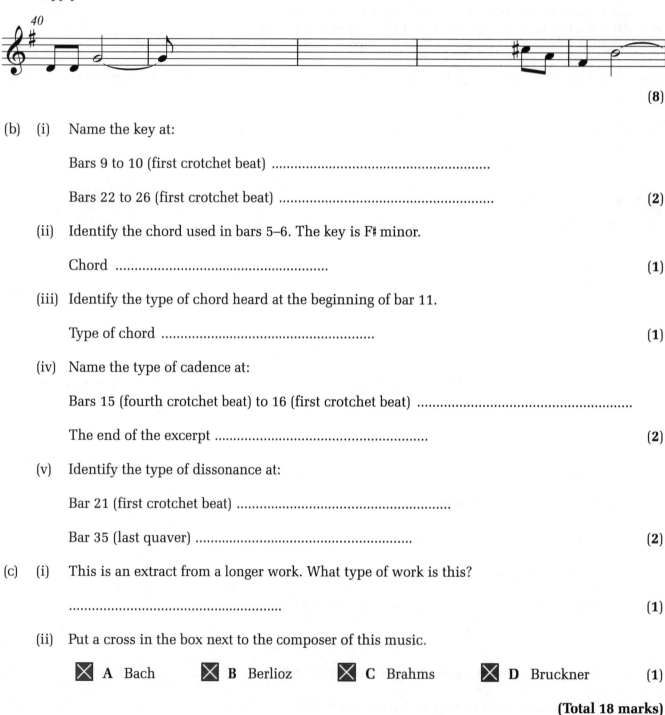

                                                                            (8)

(b)   (i)   Name the key at:

             Bars 9 to 10 (first crotchet beat) ....

             Bars 22 to 26 (first crotchet beat) ....   **(2)**

      (ii)   Identify the chord used in bars 5–6. The key is F♯ minor.

             Chord ....   **(1)**

      (iii) Identify the type of chord heard at the beginning of bar 11.

             Type of chord ....   **(1)**

      (iv)   Name the type of cadence at:

             Bars 15 (fourth crotchet beat) to 16 (first crotchet beat) ....

             The end of the excerpt ....   **(2)**

      (v)   Identify the type of dissonance at:

             Bar 21 (first crotchet beat) ....

             Bar 35 (last quaver) ....   **(2)**

(c)   (i)   This is an extract from a longer work. What type of work is this?

             ....   **(1)**

      (ii)   Put a cross in the box next to the composer of this music.

             ☒ **A** Bach   ☒ **B** Berlioz   ☒ **C** Brahms   ☒ **D** Bruckner   **(1)**

                                                                            (Total 18 marks)

Test 3   **Track 35**

You will hear an excerpt of music five times. The playings will be separated by pauses as indicated on page 37.

There is a skeleton score on page 22 of the score insert, which you must follow as you listen to the music for this test.

(a)   Complete the melody line of bars 19–20. You may work in rough on the skeleton score, but you must copy your answer onto the stave below.

(8)

(b)   (i)   Through what key does the music pass in bars 4 (third quaver beat) to 5 (first quaver beat)?

       ....   **(1)**

       (ii)   Identify the key in the marked passage from bars 16–17.

       ....   **(1)**

       (iii) Name the key and type of cadence at the end of the excerpt.

       Key ....

       Cadence ....   **(2)**

       (iv) Identify the chords in:

       Bar 8 (first dotted-crotchet beat) ....

       Bar 17 (second dotted-crotchet beat) ....   **(2)**

       (v)   What type of chord is heard three times in the marked passage from bars 23–24?

       ....   **(1)**

       (vi) What type of dissonance is heard at each of the three locations indicated by arrows in bars 10–13?

       ....   **(1)**

(c)   (i)   The excerpt is from a four-movement sonata. Which movement is it most likely to be from?

       ....   **(1)**

       (ii)   Put a cross in the box next to the composer of this music.

       ☒ **A** Beethoven   ☒ **B** Corelli   ☒ **C** Mozart   ☒ **D** Shostakovich   **(1)**

(Total 18 marks)

Test 4   **Track 36**

You will hear an excerpt of music five times. The playings will be separated by pauses as indicated on page 37.

There is a skeleton score on page 23 of the score insert, which you must follow as you listen to the music for this test.

(a)   Write out the melody line of bars 6 (second crotchet) to 8 (third quaver). You may work in rough on the skeleton score, but you must copy your answer onto the stave below.

                                                                                                        (8)

(b)   (i)   Identify the keys and cadences in bars 14 and 24–25.

             Bar 14:   Key ....

                             Cadence ....

             Bars 24–25: Key ....

                             Cadence ....   (4)

       (ii)   Identify the key in bar 21.

             ....   (1)

       (iii) Name the type of dissonance used in bar 9.

             ....   (1)

       (iv)   Precisely describe the harmonic device used in bars 10–12.

             ....   (1)

(c)   (i)   From what type of work is this excerpt taken?

             ....   (1)

       (ii)   Put a cross in the box next to the composer of this music.

             ☒ **A** Corelli   ☒ **B** Dowland   ☒ **C** Handel   ☒ **D** Purcell   (1)

       (iii) Put a cross in the box next to the year in which this music was composed.

             ☒ **A** 1592   ☒ **B** 1642   ☒ **C** 1692   ☒ **D** 1742   (1)

                                                                                     (Total 18 marks)

Section B: Music in Context

Section B of the Unit 6 paper deals with the set works for Area of Study 3: Applied Music. You will find the works for the year of your examination listed in the requirements for Unit 6 in the specification.

Section B will contain three questions, of which you have to answer any two. They will be labelled 3 (a), 3 (b) and 3 (c), and each will refer to a different set work. In each case you will be asked to identify particular musical features and indicate how these help to place the piece in its social and historical context.

Answers may be written in note form (bullet points, etc.), in continuous prose, or indeed in some mixture of the two. You may find that use of continuous prose helps you to express your meaning most clearly and fully, and it is a useful preparation for Section C, where this form of writing must be used. Whatever your style of writing, make sure that everything is legible, correct in terms of spelling, punctuation and grammar, intelligible and well organised: you will be assessed on the 'quality of written communication'.

Remember to:

1. Answer the question

    ➤ Include everything that you consider is relevant, even if it seems obvious
    ➤ Avoid everything that is irrelevant, even if it is correct.

2. Give an example if at all possible, whenever you make a point

    ➤ An example nearly always requires a bar reference. For example, if your point is 'The composer uses diminished 7th chords,' add 'as in bar 34, beat 2'. (You will have an unmarked copy of the anthology in the exam to allow you to look up bar references.)

The specimen questions below give you some idea of the way these questions are framed. For sample answers, see page 66.

> Additional information on answering this type of question (and Section C questions) is available in the *Edexcel A2 Music Revision Guide 3rd Edition* (Rhinegold Education, 2014).

2015

What features of instrumentation, harmony and tonality would enable you to establish a date of composition for Gabrieli's *Sonata pian'e forte* (*NAM* 14)? **(13)**

2016

ET: Flying Theme (*NAM* 45) accompanies a depiction of an aerial bike-ride. What features of the score make it particularly suitable for this purpose? **(13)**

2017

To what extent can the 'Vivo' from Stravinsky's *Pulcinella Suite* (*NAM* 7) be regarded as an example of neo-classicism in music? **(13)**

Section C: Continuity and Change in Instrumental Music

Section C of the Unit 6 paper deals with the set works from Area of Study 1: Instrumental Music. Note that these are different from the ones you studied for Unit 3 (at AS level). You will find the works for the year of your examination listed in the requirements for Unit 6 in the specification.

Section C will contain two questions, of which you have to answer only one. They will be labelled 4 (a) and 4 (b). Each option in the specimen Question 4 that was published when the specification was launched deals with three works, and we have assumed in this book that this will be the pattern in the actual exam. Each option in Question 4 will focus on one or more named musical features, asking you to demonstrate how these help us to see continuity and change from one work to another. Discussion will be limited to the named works – it is not necessary to refer to works from outside the anthology.

Answers must be essays written in continuous prose, and quality of written communication will be assessed. As in Section B, make sure that everything is legible, correct in terms of spelling, punctuation and grammar, intelligible and well organised. As your answer will be in essay form, you may wish to include an introductory paragraph and a concluding one, rather than just starting straight in with relevant information as you might in Section B. But to be worthwhile, an introduction or a conclusion must do more than just repeat what is written in the body of the essay.

The specimen questions below give you some idea of the way these questions are framed. For sample answers, see pages 67–69.

2015

Beethoven: Septet in E♭, Op. 20, movement I (*NAM* 17)
Louis Armstrong and his Hot Five: *West End Blues* (*NAM* 48)
Tippett: Concerto for Double String Orchestra, movement I (*NAM* 6)

Compare and contrast melody and harmony in the three pieces listed above. **(36)**

2016

Haydn: Symphony No. 26 in D minor, movement I (*NAM* 2)
Brahms: Piano Quintet in F minor, Op. 34, movement III (*NAM* 18)
Duke Ellington and his Orchestra: *Black and Tan Fantasy* (*NAM* 49)

Compare and contrast instrumentation and textures in the above works. **(36)**

2017

Shostakovich: String Quartet No. 8, Op. 110, movement I (*NAM* 9)
Cage: Sonatas and Interludes for Prepared Piano, Sonatas I–III (*NAM* 10)
Corelli: Trio Sonata in D, Op. 3, No. 2, movement IV (*NAM* 15)

Compare and contrast approaches to melody, rhythm and metre in the three works listed above. **(36)**

Answers and how to mark them

Note that, in the following mark schemes, letters, words or phrases in parentheses are not essential: for example 'pizz(icato)' means that you get the mark for 'pizzicato' in full or the abbreviation 'pizz.'. Numbers in parentheses are numbers of marks to be awarded. An oblique stroke (/) separates alternative correct solutions. Letters, words or phrases which are underlined are essential: you don't get the mark without them.

If you ever provide *correct and relevant* information that is not listed below – for no mark scheme is completely comprehensive – you can receive credit for this. Ask your teacher if you are in doubt.

Question 1: Comparison (2015)

Test 1

Excerpt A: Vivaldi's Concerto in D minor, Op. 3, No. 11, movement II
Excerpt B: movement III

The work from which these excerpts are taken is one of twelve concertos published by Antonio Vivaldi (1678–1741) as *L'Estro Armonico* in Amsterdam in 1711, one of the most ambitious publishing ventures of the time, clearly aimed at spreading his music beyond Italy. Unlike many works in this collection, which were written for various solo combinations ranging from a single violin up to four violins and cello, the concerto in D minor chiefly employs the typical Corelli concertino of two violins and cello. Excerpt A is the opening of the second (slow) movement, which is in the manner of a siciliana. Excerpt B has the opening bars of the finale, with the vigorous string writing so characteristic of many quick movements by Vivaldi.

Related set works: Corelli's Trio Sonata in D, Op. 3, No. 2, movement IV (*NAM* 15) – Italian music of the mid to late Baroque; Tippett's Concerto for Double String Orchestra, movement I (*NAM* 6) – concerto.

(a) Excerpt A: full strings <u>at first</u> (1), then <u>solo</u> violin (with legato melody) (1) plus <u>upper</u> strings (with detached chords) (1). Excerpt B: concertino/solo group (entering in imitation) <u>at first</u> (1) of two violins and cello (1) then with ripieno/accompanying group (1). Max. 3.

(b) Concerto (grosso) (1). *Note:* both excerpts are from a concerto grosso, but the first includes a substantial passage for a solo violin, rather in the manner of a solo concerto, so that the answer 'concerto' without the adjective 'grosso' is acceptable. The dividing line between the different types of concerto was not always clear cut in Baroque times.

(c) Excerpt A: melody-dominated homophony (1), accompanied by repeated chords (1). Excerpt B: imitative (at first) (1); (solo cello with) accompaniment of detached chords (1); solo violins in 3rds (1). Max. 2.

(d) (i) TRUE (1); (ii) TRUE (1)

(e) D – Vivaldi (1)

(f) Accept any year between 1690 and 1750 (1)

Test 2

Excerpt A: Beethoven's *Fidelio*, Act 1, No. 4 ('Hat man nicht auch Gold beineben')
Excerpt B: Act 1, No. 7 ('Ha! welch' ein Augenblick!')

Fidelio by Ludwig van Beethoven (1770–1827) belongs to a type of opera popular at the start of the 19th century in which the plot hinges on a rescue. Florestan is a political prisoner saved by his wife Leonora (who disguises herself as a boy, Fidelio). There is a scene of great poignancy at the beginning of Act 2, where Florestan, still in chains, sings of his pain, loneliness and imminent death. Florestan's desperate situation at that point might remind us to some small degree of Dido's in Act 3 of Purcell's *Dido and Aeneas*. Listen to Florestan's aria (from

Act 2 of *Fidelio*) and Dido's lament (from Act 3 of *Dido and Aeneas*), and try comparing and contrasting the two composers' methods of depicting extremes of grief and desolation.

Related set works: 'Thy hand, Belinda' and 'When I am laid in earth' from Purcell's *Dido and Aeneas* (*NAM* 36) – opera; Beethoven's Septet in E♭, Op. 20, movement I (*NAM* 17) – music of Beethoven.

(a)   C (1)

(b)   Excerpt A is mostly limited in range/Excerpt B has wider range (1) and is (often) higher (1). Award (1) for any additional point about specific intervals, e.g. diminished 7th, octave and augmented 2nd. Phrasing in Excerpt A is periodic, phrasing in Excerpt B is irregular (1). Max. 2.

(c)   Excerpt A begins at a moderate(ly fast) speed (Allegro moderato) (1), slows to a pause (1), then becomes quicker (Allegro) (1), before ending with a final rall./rit. (1). Excerpt B is fast <u>throughout</u> (Allegro agitato) (1). Max. 2.

(d)   Diminished 7th chords (1); augmented 6th chords (1); dominant (minor) 9ths/diminished 7th chords <u>above</u> dominant in bass (1); augmented triad (heard once) (1). Max. 2.

(e)   Opera (1)

(f)   C – 1805 (1)

(g)   A – Beethoven (1)

Test 3

Excerpt A: Stravinsky's Symphony in C, movement I
Excerpt B: movement IV

Igor Stravinsky (1882–1971) composed his Symphony in C in 1940 during the neoclassical phase of his career, which included *Pulcinella*, composed some 20 years previously. The symphony is not closely based on originals by other composers as *Pulcinella* was, but there is a debt to the past in the continued use of tonality (at a time when the way forward musically appeared to be increasingly atonal and serial), in a kind of emotional restraint which has clearer parallels in the Classical period than in Romantic music, and in apparent echoes of the celebrated four-note motif from Beethoven's Symphony No. 5.

Related set works: 'Sinfonia', 'Gavotta' and 'Vivo' from Stravinsky's *Pulcinella Suite* (*NAM* 7) *and* Tippett's Concerto for Double String Orchestra, movement I (*NAM* 6) – neoclassicism.

(a)   G (1)

(b)   Repeats whole figure (immediately, or from time to time within oboe melody)/alters intervals but not overall shape (e.g. to D, E, B)/sounds repeated Bs only (e.g. in timpani near beginning)/(rhythmic) augmentation (in bass or melody) (1).

(c)   (Mostly) stepwise (1) and within narrow (low) range (1); <u>opening</u> (three-note) <u>rising</u> pattern (1) inverted (1); a few leaps (1) including (perfect) 5ths (1). Max. 2. *Note*: reference to the two simultaneous melodic lines is more to do with texture than melodic writing, and need not be included here.

(d)   Oboe (1)

(e)   (Two) bassoon(s) (1) plus horns and/or trombones (1); (melody-dominated) homophony (1) with two simultaneous melodies (1) accompanied by detached chords (1). Max. 3.

(f)   Stravinsky (1). Accept instead any other composer of neoclassical orchestral music active in the middle years of the 20th century, e.g. Prokofiev, Tippett.

(g)   B – 1940 (1)

Test 4

Excerpt A: *Three Blind Mice* by Morehouse and Trumbauer
Excerpt B: *Krazy Kat* by Morehouse and Trumbauer

Both excerpts feature the celebrated American jazz-cornet player Bix Beiderbecke (1903–1931), one of the first white jazz musicians to be highly regarded by black players. It was towards the end of the 20th century that Beiderbecke's full stature became apparent: this was aided by the appearance of the 1990 film *Bix: an interpretation of a legend*. Both excerpts are examples of Dixieland jazz, a type of traditional jazz that was based on the New Orleans style of the early 20th century.

Related set work: *West End Blues* by Louis Armstrong and his Hot Five (*NAM* 48) – early 20th-century jazz and blues.

(a)   Syncopation (1); swung rhythms (1)

(b)   Excerpt A (1)

(c)   Excerpt A: chordal/homophonic (1); reed(s)/sax(es) (1) in antiphony/call and response/alternation (1) with solo piano (1). Excerpt B: melody on cornet (1) accompanied by <u>detached</u> chords (1) on sax(es) (1). Max. 4.

(d)   Violin (1)

(e)   B – Traditional jazz (1)

(f)   B – 1927 (1)

Question 1: Comparison (2016)

Test 1

Excerpt A: Handel's *Let God Arise*, HWV 256b, movement III
Excerpt B: movement IV

Anthems sung by present-day church choirs are usually fairly short pieces for choir and organ. Anthems by George Frideric Handel (1685–1759), composed after he had settled in England in the 1710s, are in several movements, include soloists as well as choir, and have orchestral accompaniment. Therefore in some ways they are similar to Bach's cantatas, but the texts are in English and chorales are not used. *Let God Arise* was originally written while Handel was composer to the Duke of Chandos, and is one of 12 'Chandos anthems'. The later version, on which this test is based, was revised for performance in King George I's Chapel Royal.

Related set work: Bach's Cantata No. 48, movements I–IV (*NAM* 28) – late Baroque choral music.

(a)   (Male) alto/countertenor (1) and bass/baritone (1) soloists (1). Max. 2.

(b)   Four-part (1) chorus/choir (1) including boys' voices/of boys' and men's voices (1). Max. 2.

(c)   Oboe (1)

(d)   Excerpt A: dialogue/imitation between solo parts (supported by continuo/bass)/duet plus accompaniment (1). Excerpt B: begins with octaves in choir (accompanied by bass) (1); where 'Hallelujah' begins texture is homophonic/chordal/antiphonal (1), followed by contrapuntal/imitative/fugal texture (1). Max. 2.

(e)   Anthem (1). Allow oratorio.

(f)   Handel (1). Allow Arne, Boyce or Purcell.

(g)   B – 1726 (1)

Test 2

Excerpt A: Schubert's Symphony No. 5, movement III
Excerpt B: Schubert's Symphony No. 9 (the 'Great C major'), movement III

Symphony No. 5 by Franz Schubert (1797–1828) is an early work (1816), whereas the 'Great C major' was written towards the end of the composer's short life. No. 5, like some symphonies by Haydn and Mozart, uses a smallish orchestra without clarinets, timpani or brass other than horns. It still has a Minuet as the third movement (although, contrary to Classical practice, this is in the relative minor – an instance of Schubert's growing tonal freedom). The third movement of No. 9 is a Scherzo, a sign of Beethoven's influence, and indeed the work as a whole could not have been conceived without the example of that composer.

Related set works: Haydn's Symphony No. 26 in D minor, movement I (*NAM* 2) – symphony; Brahms' Piano Quintet in F minor, Op. 34, movement III (*NAM* 18) – scherzo.

(a)   In octaves (1); full orchestra/tutti/strings with woodwind and horns/brass (1)

(b)   (i) In octaves (also) (1); (ii) strings only (1)

(c)   Clarinet(s) (1)

(d)   Excerpt B starts/ends/is in a major key (1). Excerpt B ends in the dominant (not the tonic as in Excerpt A) (1); Excerpt A modulates to the relative major (1). Excerpt A visits only closely related keys (1), but Excerpt B passes through a more distant/(less closely related) (major) key (on the flattened leading note) (1). Excerpt B is more diatonic/lacks the (descending) (semitonal) chromatic movement in Excerpt A (1). Max. 2.

(e)   Scherzo (1)

(f)   Symphony (1)

(g)   C – Schubert (1)

Test 3

Excerpt A: Act 1, No. 5 ('Maria') from Bernstein's *West Side Story*
Excerpt B: Act 2, No. 15 ('A Boy Like That')

Leonard Bernstein (1918–1990), a composer, conductor, pianist and teacher, was immensely versatile – equally at home in classical and popular styles. The plot of his celebrated musical *West Side Story* has much in common with Shakespeare's *Romeo and Juliet* (love transcends social rivalries, but with tragic results). In Excerpt A, Tony, a leading member of the Jets, is in love with Maria, sister of Bernardo, leader of the opposing gang, the Sharks. In Excerpt B, Anita (Bernardo's girlfriend) warns Maria against Tony. For more on *West Side Story*, see *Musicals in Focus* by Paul Terry (Rhinegold Education, second edition 2009).

Related set work: Bernstein's *On the Waterfront: Symphonic Suite* (opening) (*NAM* 43) – another example of the composer's versatility, this was originally music for film.

(a)   Excerpt A begins on a monotone/has repeated notes (1), Excerpt B has a wider range/includes lower notes (1). Excerpt A is diatonic, Excerpt B has some chromatic notes (1). Max. 2.

(b)   Excerpt A is in simple duple/quadruple time (throughout) (1), with (frequent) triplets (1). In Excerpt B the time signature alternates (1) between (simple) duple/quadruple and triple (1) (accept instead 'irregular metre'). Excerpt B has more frequent rests/shorter phrases/is more disjointed (1). (Prominent) habanera rhythm in (second half of) Excerpt A (1), with cross rhythms (between this and the triplets) (1). Syncopation in Excerpt B (1). Max. 3.

(c) Excerpt A: major key/(upward) (tertiary) modulation or key shift/with raised fourth/Lydian inflections (1). Excerpt B: minor key/with some touches of major/tonal ambiguity (1).

(d) Musical (1)

(e) C – 1957 (1)

(f) A – Bernstein (1)

Test 4

Excerpt A: 'Pagodes' from Debussy's *Estampes*
Excerpt B: 'Jimbo's Lullaby' from Debussy's *Children's Corner*

'Pagodes' by Claude Debussy (1862–1918) is the first of the three *Estampes* ('Engravings') – a title that underlines the close relationship in Debussy's mind between the visual arts and music. Pagodas are those tall towers in Asia with several storeys, each storey having a projecting roof with upturned eaves. Debussy first became aware of music from Southeast Asia, including gamelan, at the 1889 Exposition Universelle (a kind of world fair) in Paris. *Children's Corner* is a suite of pieces written partly for the delight of Debussy's young daughter Claude-Emma. Jimbo (perhaps a misspelling of Jumbo) was her toy elephant: the low opening bars capture the animal's awkward movements perfectly.

Related set works: Sarabande and Gigue from Bach's Partita No. 4 in D, BWV 828 (*NAM* 21); Shostakovich's Prelude and Fugue in A, Op. 87, No.7 (*NAM* 25) – examples of keyboard music, both earlier and later.

(a) C – Pentatonic (1). *Note*: in both excerpts the melody often employs only *four* notes from the pentatonic scale (the second, third, fourth and fifth – thereby avoiding the tonic), just as some gamelan melodies tend to favour four pitches from a five-note *slendro* scale.

(b) Both use non-functional harmony (1), avoiding triads and their inversions (1). Chords are often built up from notes of the pentatonic scale (1), with major 2nds (1) prominent especially in Excerpt B (1). Harmonic rhythm/rate of chord change slow (1). Excerpt A has (double) pedal/tonic-and-dominant drone (at start) (1); Excerpt B has repeated, low tonic notes towards end (1). Max. 3.

(c) Melody-dominated homophony (1), with melody at top (to start with) (1). Later melody (with longer notes) in middle of texture (1) in octaves (1), under (octave) triplets (1). Max. 2.

(d) Monophonic/monophony (1)

(e) Gamelan/Balinese/Javanese (1)

(f) B – 1900s (1)

(g) Debussy (1). Accept instead Ravel.

Question 1: Comparison (2017)

Test 1

Excerpt A: Shostakovich's Symphony No. 9, Op. 70, movement I
Excerpt B: movement IV

Dmitri Shostakovich (1906–1975) completed his Symphony No. 9, Op. 70 in 1945 and it received its first performance in November of the same year in Leningrad. Its generally humorous, neoclassical vein caused some consternation, as it was expected that Shostakovich would produce an epic work in the same mould as the seventh and eighth symphonies to celebrate Soviet victory over the Nazis. The first excerpt used here is almost the whole of the exposition from the sonata-form first movement (Allegro), its brevity characteristic of the reduced scale of the work. The darker second excerpt is the opening of the Largo which separates the scherzo and finale.

Related set works: 'Sinfonia', 'Gavotta' and 'Vivo' from Stravinsky's *Pulcinella Suite* (*NAM* 7) – neoclassicism; Berlioz's *Harold in Italy*, movement I (*NAM* 3) – symphony.

(a)   (Suspended) cymbal (1)

(b)   Excerpt A is quicker/Excerpt B is slower (1); A is in a steady tempo throughout/B is freer in tempo (1). B makes use of dotted rhythm <u>at the opening</u> (1). Max. 2.

(c)   Bassoon (1)

(d)   Excerpt A's melodic line initially falls, whereas Excerpt B's rises (1); A opens with a broken chord followed by a scale, whereas B is mainly conjunct (1); A has a relatively wide range, while B spans only a 5th (1); A contains a trill (1); A is major, whereas B is minor (1). Max. 3.

(e)   Symphony (1)

(f)   C – Shostakovich (1)

(g)   1945; accept any year between 1920 and 1975 (1)

Test 2

Excerpt A: Monteverdi's *Vespers* (Magnificat, 'Deposuit potentes')
Excerpt B: Monteverdi's *Vespers* (Magnificat, 'Suscepit Israel')

These two excerpts are taken from the Magnificat in Monteverdi's *Vespers* (published in Venice in 1610). Monteverdi was eventually appointed to the post of maestro di cappella at St. Mark's in 1613, and the *Vespers* provide some of the finest examples of the early Baroque concertato style associated with Venetian composers (see Gabrieli's *In ecclesiis*). The excerpts show how Monteverdi combined a sacred cantus firmus (the plainsong melody sung in long notes by the tenor) with the more complex vocal and instrumental elaborations typical of his operatic style.

Related set works: Gabrieli's *In ecclesiis* (*NAM* 27) and Sweelinck's *Pavana Lachrimae* (*NAM* 20) – both dating from the same era. Gabrieli's work is also an example of Venetian concertato music.

(a)   Cornett(s) (1); violin(s) (1)

(b)   Both have (essentially) the same (tenor) melody/cantus firmus (1) in long notes (1). The same continuo instruments are used/organ is used in both (1) plus chitarrone/theorbo/large or bass lute (1). Dotted rhythms are used in both (1). Max. 3.

(c)   Excerpt A has antiphony/dialogue (between cornetts) (1); Excerpt B has imitation (1). Voices: A has tenor(s)/male voice(s) only *or* B <u>also</u> has sopranos/women's voices (1). Instruments: while A uses (obbligato) instruments/cornetts/violins, B is for (voices and) continuo only (1). A repeatedly uses scales (1). B has (much) melisma (1). Rhythms in B are frequently more complex/florid *or* use shorter/quicker notes (1). Max. 3.

(d)   B – 1600–1630 (1)

(e)   C – Monteverdi (1)

Test 3

Excerpt A: Walton's *Henry V* ('Prologue')
Excerpt B: Walton's *Henry V* ('Agincourt Song' from 'Epilogue')

Walton's score for Olivier's film of Shakespeare's *Henry V* was composed in 1943–44. The first excerpt accompanied the opening shots of medieval London, the passage for wordless chorus underscoring tracking shots of the Thames from the Tower of London to the Globe Theatre (where the play was probably first performed in about 1600). In the epilogue, Walton used a version of the 'Agincourt song' originally composed to celebrate Henry's victory over the French in 1415.

Related set works: Auric's *Passport to Pimlico:* 'The Siege of Burgundy' (*NAM* 42) and Pheloung's *Morse on the Case* (*NAM* 46) – examples of incidental music. Auric's score dates from the same decade as Walton's.

(a)   Excerpt A uses male and female voices *or* Excerpt B uses male voices <u>only</u> (1). A is wordless/uses vocalisation (1); in B words are sung (1). In A the voices are used purely for colour (1); in B they carry the main melody (1). Max. 3.

(b)   (i) Flute (and/or harp) (1); (ii) cymbals (1)

(c)   (i) True (1); (ii) false (1); (iii) false (1)

(d)   D – Walton (1)

(e)   1944; accept any year between 1930 and 1980 (1)

Test 4

Excerpt A: Schubert's String Quartet in D minor ('Death and the Maiden'), movement IV
Excerpt B: Schubert's Octet in F major, movement VI

Both these chamber works were completed in March 1824. The Quartet is known as 'Death and the Maiden' because Schubert used the music from his song of this name as the basis for the variations that form the quartet's second movement. Excerpt B comes from the opening of the finale of Schubert's six-movement Octet. In spite of the dark-toned quality of this excerpt, the Octet as a whole harks back to the relaxed serenade or divertimento style of the mid- to late-18th century. For another example of the genre, see Beethoven's Septet (*NAM* 17).

Related set works: Corelli's Trio Sonata in D, Op. 3, No. 2, movement IV (*NAM* 15) – an example of chamber music; Mozart's Piano Sonata in B♭, K. 333, movement I (*NAM* 22) – an example of an earlier Viennese Classical style.

(a)   Clarinet (1), bassoon (1), horn (1), double bass (1). Max. 2.

(b)   Tremolo (1)

(c)   Excerpt A opens in/has many octaves (1), with chords at the ends of (some) phrases (1). Limited use of imitation (viola and cello) (1). Excerpt B alternates (1) octaves (1) with homophonic passages (1). Max. 3.

(d)   Excerpt A is in compound duple time (⁶/₈) (1); Excerpt B is in simple quadruple time (⁴/₄) (allow any form of simple duple or quadruple) (1). A uses (many) crotchet-quaver/long-short pairs (1); B uses (many) (double-)dotted rhythms (1). Credit additional details. Max. 2.

(e)   D – Schubert (1)

(f)   C – 1824 (1)

Dictation exercises

Test 1

11 note values to be supplied. Starting key: G major. If desired, the tonic chord (G–B–D) can be sounded before one or more playings of the test.

Handel: Minuet from *Alcina*, bars 9–16

Test 2

12 pitches to be supplied. Starting key: F major. See direction for Test 1 on possible use of tonic chord.

Samuel Wesley: Gavotte in F, opening

Test 3

7 note values and 6 pitches to be supplied. Starting key: D major.

Mozart: Piano Concerto in D minor, K. 466, mvt. III, bars 396–403

Test 4

9 note values and 13 pitches to be supplied. Starting key: F major.

Haydn: String Quartet in C major, Op.33 No. 3, mvt. III, opening

Test 5

9 pitches and 7 note values to be supplied. Starting key: A major.

Schubert: 'Frühlingstraum' from *Die schöne Müllerin*, bars 4–14

Test 6

10 notes to be supplied. Starting key: E♭ major.

Beethoven: Quintet in E flat,
Op. 16, mvt. III, bars 8–17

Test 7

9 notes and 1 pitch to be supplied. Starting key: B minor.

Mendelssohn: *Lieder ohne Worte,*
Op. 67 No. 5 in B minor, bars 9–13

Test 8

11 notes to be supplied. Starting key: G major.

Albrechtsberger:
Neue Leichte Praeludien, No. 5, ending

Test 9

12 notes to be supplied. Starting key: E minor.

Schumann: *Album für die Jugend,*
Op. 68 No. 16, ending

Test 10

11 notes to be supplied. Starting key: A major.

Corelli: Sonata in A major,
Op. 5 No. 9, Preludio, opening

Test 11

11 notes to be supplied. Starting key: C minor.

Beethoven: Sonata in C minor,
Op. 13, mvt. II, opening

Test 12

12 notes to be supplied. Starting key: F major.

Haydn: Divertimento (Keyboard Sonata) in F,
Hob. XVI:9, mvt. II, bars 19–25

Test 13

13 notes to be supplied. Starting key: E minor. *Note the diminished 7th chord outline in bars 5–6.*

Vivaldi: Cello Sonata in E minor,
RV 40, mvt. IV, bars 44–54

Test 14

11 notes to be supplied. Starting key: D minor.

Buxtehude: Canzona in D minor,
BuxWV168, bars 66–69

Test 15

12 notes to be supplied. Starting key: D major.

Mendelssohn: *Lieder ohne Worte,*
Op. 85 No 4 in D, bars 20–24

Test 16

9 notes to be supplied. Starting key: C major.

Schubert: 'Halt' from
Die schöne Müllerin, bars 11–19

Test 17

10 notes to be supplied. Starting key: E minor.

Chopin: Nocturne, Op. 72
No. 1, bars 9–13

Test 18

12 notes to be supplied. Starting key: D minor.

Krebs (formerly attrib. J.S. Bach): Fugue from
Prelude and Fugue in D minor, BWV 554, bars 6–9

Test 19

10 notes to be supplied. Starting key: A♭ major.

Vierne: 'Lied' from *24 Pièces en style libre*,
Op. 31, opening

Test 20

11 notes to be supplied. Starting key: E minor.

Reger: 'Elegie' from *Bunte Blätter*,
Op. 36 No. 6, ending

Test 21

12 notes to be supplied. Starting key: E♭ major.

Traditional

Question 2: Aural Awareness (2015)

Test 1

Excerpt: Haydn's Symphony No. 101 in D, movement I

Symphony No. 101 in D major ('The Clock') was composed by Joseph Haydn (1732–1809) as one of a set of 'London' symphonies for his visit to England in 1794. The slow introduction, which is in the tonic minor key, helps to throw into relief the cheerful dance-like melody in ⁶⁄₈ time that heads the main part of the movement. This is subtly linked to the Adagio by the rising scale with which each section begins. The nickname 'The Clock' was applied to the symphony because of the ticking effect of the pizzicato strings and staccato bassoons in the second movement.

Related set works: Haydn's String Quartet in E♭, Op. 33, No. 2, movement IV (*NAM* 16) *and* Beethoven's Septet in E♭, Op. 20, movement I (*NAM* 17) – music in the Classical style.

(a)

There are 10 pitches and 10 note lengths to complete.

0	No work offered
1	1–2 pitches and/or note lengths correct
2	3–4 pitches and/or note lengths correct
3	5–7 pitches and/or note lengths correct
4	8–10 pitches and/or note lengths correct
5	11–13 pitches and note lengths correct
6	14–16 pitches and note lengths correct
7	17–18 pitches and note lengths correct
8	19–20 pitches and note lengths correct

(b) (i) Chord A: Ic/tonic second inversion (1); chord B: V/dominant (1)

(ii) Bars 11–12: F major/relative major (1), perfect (1); bars 21–23: D minor/tonic (1), imperfect (1)

(iii) Diminished seventh (1)

(c) (i) Symphony (1)

(ii) D – Haydn (1)

(iii) Any year between 1770 and 1809 (1)

Test 2

Excerpt: Mozart's Piano Concerto No. 23 in A, K. 488, movement II

The music is from the second movement of Piano Concerto No. 23 in A (K. 488) by Wolfgang Amadeus Mozart (1756–1791), composed in 1786. Mozart was the earliest important composer of piano concertos, and to this day probably the most prolific. The solo parts, composed for himself to play, are not virtuosic in the manner of most 19th-century concertos, partly because late 18th-century instruments were far less strong in sound and construction than their successors. Accordingly the orchestra is also smaller, with the most powerful passages reserved for sections where there is no solo part. Mozart appears to have accompanied the orchestra in continuo fashion (especially where the piano part has only a single bass line), and he probably embellished or otherwise built on the notated solo part elsewhere. This test opens with a passage for piano solo, based on a lilting melody in ⁶⁄₈ time, almost in a pastoral style, but in an emotionally tense F♯ minor. The expected move to A major (the relative major) begins in bar 25; the shift to A *minor* shortly afterwards is both magical and slightly chilling.

Related set works: Tippett's Concerto for Double String Orchestra, movement I (*NAM* 6) – concerto; Haydn's String Quartet in E♭, Op. 33, No. 2, movement IV (*NAM* 16) *and* Beethoven's Septet in E♭, Op. 20, movement I (*NAM* 17) – music in the Classical style.

(a)

There are 11 pitches and 11 note lengths to complete.

0	No work offered
1	1–2 pitches and/or note lengths correct
2	3–5 pitches and/or note lengths correct
3	6–8 pitches and/or note lengths correct
4	9–11 pitches and/or note lengths correct
5	12–14 pitches and note lengths correct
6	15–17 pitches and note lengths correct
7	18–20 pitches and note lengths correct
8	21–22 pitches and note lengths correct

(b) (i) Bar 6: appoggiatura (1); bar 14: suspension (1)

(ii) Chord A: Neapolitan sixth (1); chord B: Ic/tonic second inversion (1); chord C: V⁷/dominant seventh (1)

(iii) A major/relative major (1)

(iv) Imperfect (1)

(c) (i) (Piano) concerto (1)

(ii) D – Mozart (1)

(iii) B – 1786 (1)

Test 3

Excerpt: 'Kommt ein schlanker Bursch gegangen' from Weber's *Der Freischütz*

This test is based on an excerpt from *Der Freischütz* (a title sometimes translated as 'The Marksman' or 'The Freeshooter') by Carl Maria von Weber (1786–1826). This work, commonly referred to as an opera, may also be called a *Singspiel*, a type of opera with German text and spoken dialogue between the musical numbers, of which Mozart's *Die Zauberflöte* ('The Magic Flute', 1791) is the best-known example. Our excerpt is the beginning of a song from Act II sung by the principal female character, Agathe. It is labelled 'arietta', meaning an operatic song that is shorter and/or lighter and less elaborate than a fully-fledged aria. *Der Freischütz* is an early example of Romanticism in music, as is demonstrated above all in the celebrated 'Wolf's Glen scene' (end of Act II) with its stunning depiction of the supernatural.

Related set work: 'Thy hand, Belinda' and 'When I am laid in earth' from Purcell's *Dido and Aeneas* (*NAM* 36) – opera.

(a)

There are 9 pitches and 9 note lengths to complete.

0	No work offered
1	1–2 pitches and/or note lengths correct
2	3–4 pitches and/or note lengths correct
3	5–6 pitches and/or note lengths correct
4	7–9 pitches and/or note lengths correct
5	10–12 pitches and note lengths correct
6	13–14 pitches and note lengths correct
7	15–16 pitches and note lengths correct
8	17–18 pitches and note lengths correct

(b) (i) Chord A: diminished seventh (1); chord B: dominant seventh (1)

    (ii) F major/subdominant (1)

    (iii) Bars 43–44: perfect (1), G major/dominant (1); bars 54–55: imperfect (1), A minor/relative minor (1)

(c) (i) Opera/Singspiel (1)

    (ii) D – Weber (1)

    (iii) D – 1821 (1)

Test 4

Excerpt: 'Domine Deus, Agnus Dei' from Vivaldi's *Gloria*

Test 4 is based on 'Domine Deus, Agnus Dei' ('Lord God, Lamb of God'), from the celebrated D major *Gloria* (RV 589) by Antonio Vivaldi (1678–1741). 'Gloria [in excelsis Deo]' ('Glory to God in the highest') is a Latin text from the principal Roman Catholic service, the Mass. While it was frequently set as the second movement of a multi-movement work (together with the Kyrie, Credo, Sanctus, Benedictus and Agnus Dei), Vivaldi's *Gloria* seems to have stood alone. However, it is not for his church music (nor indeed for his numerous operas) that Vivaldi is now best known. He wrote hundreds of concertos, including the so-called *Four Seasons*, helping to pioneer the three-movement (quick–slow–quick) design and ritornello form adopted by J. S. Bach, notably in the Brandenburg Concertos.

Related set works: 'Thy hand, Belinda' and 'When I am laid in earth' from Purcell's *Dido and Aeneas* (*NAM* 36) – Baroque writing for solo voice; Corelli's Trio Sonata in D, Op. 3, No. 2, movement IV (*NAM* 15) – Italian music of the mid to late Baroque.

(a)

There are 9 pitches and 9 note lengths to complete.

0	No work offered
1	1–2 pitches and/or note lengths correct
2	3–4 pitches and/or note lengths correct
3	5–6 pitches and/or note lengths correct
4	7–9 pitches and/or note lengths correct
5	10–12 pitches and note lengths correct
6	13–14 pitches and note lengths correct
7	15–16 pitches and note lengths correct
8	17–18 pitches and note lengths correct

(b) (i) Bars 8–9: D minor (1); bars 12–13: A minor (1). *Note*: in bar 8 (second minim beat) the diminished seventh (G♯–B♮–D–F) is chromatic: the G♯ and B♮ do not signify A minor.

(ii) Bar 8: diminished seventh (1); bar 11: Neapolitan sixth (1)

(iii) (Harmonic) sequence (a tone lower) (1). *Note*: Vivaldi manages to cadence in A♭ major at the end of the second passage – very far removed from the tonic key of D minor. The A♭ major chord in bar 19 does however in a sense point us ahead to the A♭ major chord at the end of bar 21, which is a Neapolitan sixth in G minor.

(iv) Perfect (1)

(v) Chord A: IVb/subdominant first inversion (1); chord B: V⁷/dominant seventh (1)

(c) (i) Mass (movement)/(a setting of) Gloria (in excelsis) (1)

(ii) D – Vivaldi (1)

Question 2: Aural Awareness (2016)

Test 1

Excerpt: Fugue from Bach's Toccata and Fugue in F, BWV 540

Test 1 is the start of the Fugue from Toccata and Fugue in F, BWV 540 by J. S. Bach (1685–1750). Earlier organ toccatas, including those by Dieterich Buxtehude (1637–1707), tended to juxtapose fugal sections and showy semi-improvisatory passages. Bach's F major Toccata is non-fugal and less obviously showy, but very challenging with its pedal solos, constant semiquaver rhythm, and passages of intricate counterpoint. The Fugue begins with a slow-moving subject characterised by an initial chromatic descent. After our excerpt ends, a different, quicker subject is introduced; the piece ends with a masterly combination of the two subjects.

Related set works: Bach's Cantata No. 48, movements I–IV (*NAM* 28) – especially movement I with its contrapuntal artifice; Bach's Partita No. 4 in D, BWV 828 (*NAM* 21) – keyboard music by Bach; Shostakovich's Prelude and Fugue in A, Op. 87, No. 7 (*NAM* 25) – fugue; Brahms' Piano Quintet in F minor, Op. 34, movement III (*NAM* 18) – fugal writing.

(a)

There are 10 pitches and 10 note lengths to complete.

0	No work offered
1	1–2 pitches and/or note lengths correct
2	3–4 pitches and/or note lengths correct
3	5–7 pitches and/or note lengths correct
4	8–10 pitches and/or note lengths correct
5	11–13 pitches and note lengths correct
6	14–16 pitches and note lengths correct
7	17–18 pitches and note lengths correct
8	19–20 pitches and note lengths correct

(b) (i) Suspension (1)

(ii) Chord A: V⁷d/dominant seventh, third inversion (1); chord B: Ib/tonic first inversion (1)

(iii) C major/dominant (1); perfect (1)

(iv) Bars 46–48: B♭ major/subdominant (1); bar 62: G minor/supertonic minor/relative minor of subdominant (1)

(v) C major/dominant (1)

(c) (i) Fugue (1)

(ii) A – J. S. Bach, 1730 (1)

Test 2

Excerpt: 'An die Nachtigall' from Brahms' *Vier Lieder*, Op. 46

'An die Nachtigall', heard in full in this test, is the last of four songs by Johannes Brahms (1833–1897) published in 1868 as his *Vier Lieder*, Op. 46. The word 'lied' (singular of 'lieder') literally means just 'song', but is applied in particular to Romantic-period art songs with German text, for solo voice and piano (or less frequently orchestral) accompaniment. The expression 'art song' not only distinguishes a lied from operatic arias, folk and popular song, but also implies a particular subtle and sophisticated relationship between voice and accompaniment, and an intimate musical response to the mood and meaning of the text. Incidentally, the songs from Schoenberg's *Pierrot Lunaire* are not usually classified as lieder, but might be 'regarded as the tradition's culmination … exacerbating the expressive possibilities of both voice and accompaniment' ('Lied' in *Grove Music Online*).

Related set works: Bach's Cantata No. 48, movements I–IV (*NAM* 28) – settings of German text; 'Der kranke Mond' from Schoenberg's *Pierrot Lunaire* (*NAM* 40) – music for solo voice; Brahms' Piano Quintet in F minor, Op. 34, movement III (*NAM* 18) – music by Brahms.

(a)

There are 12 pitches and 12 note lengths to complete.

0	No work offered
1	1–3 pitches and/or note lengths correct
2	4–6 pitches and/or note lengths correct
3	7–9 pitches and/or note lengths correct
4	10–12 pitches and/or note lengths correct
5	13–15 pitches and note lengths correct
6	16–18 pitches and note lengths correct
7	19–21 pitches and note lengths correct
8	22–24 pitches and note lengths correct

(b) (i)   II⁷b/supertonic seventh, first inversion (1)

(ii) Cadence A: imperfect (1); cadence B: interrupted (1); cadence C: plagal (1). *Note*: plagal cadences are not widely used, but here we have one of the more common usages – after an interrupted cadence, to bring a piece or section to an end. Listen to the music again, and see if you can spot another interrupted cadence, this time fairly closely followed by an imperfect cadence (in D minor, in the phrase beginning 'von neuem' at bar 30).

(iii) Bars 10–14: A major/dominant (1); bars 25–27: D major/tonic (1)

(iv) <u>Dominant</u> pedal (1)

(v)   V (1)

(c) (i)   C – Leid (1)

(ii) Brahms (1). Accept instead another early/mid 19th-century composer of lieder, such as Schumann.

Test 3

Excerpt: 'Erbarme dich, mein Gott' from Bach's *St. Matthew Passion*

The music for this test is from the alto aria 'Erbarme dich, mein Gott' ('Have pity, my God') from *St. Matthew Passion* by J. S. Bach (1685–1750). In the previous recitative Peter, Jesus' leading disciple, having just denied his master for the third time, is full of remorse and weeps bitterly. Bach then constructs a very extended aria of aching intensity on this single *Affekt*, never once cadencing in a major key. Among the expressive devices he uses are the Neapolitan sixth chord (first heard in bar 3) and some jagged melodic outlines, including augmented seconds (as in bar 5, A♯ to G♮). Bach's *St. Matthew Passion* is based on the Bible narrative of Jesus' suffering and death, but also includes non-Biblical words (such as 'Erbarme dich'). Although it is perfectly correct to call the work simply a 'Passion', the term 'oratorio Passion' is often preferred. See for example *Baroque Music in Focus* (Rhinegold Education, second edition 2010), pages 76–77.

Related set works: Bach's Cantata No. 48, movements I–IV (*NAM* 28) – Bach's music for the Lutheran church; Bach's Partita No. 4 in D, BWV 828 (*NAM* 21).

(a)

There are 11 pitches and 11 note lengths to complete.

0	No work offered
1	1–2 pitches and/or note lengths correct
2	3–5 pitches and/or note lengths correct
3	6–8 pitches and/or note lengths correct
4	9–11 pitches and/or note lengths correct
5	12–14 pitches and note lengths correct
6	15–17 pitches and note lengths correct
7	18–20 pitches and note lengths correct
8	21–22 pitches and note lengths correct

(b) (i)   Bar 4: B minor/tonic (1), imperfect (1); bar 18: F♯ minor/dominant (1), imperfect (1)

    (ii)   Chord A: IV/subdominant (1); chord B: Neapolitan sixth (1); chord C: V⁷d/dominant seventh, third inversion (1)

(c) (i)   D – Passion (1)

    (ii)   A – Bach (1)

    (iii) C – 1727 (1)

Test 4

Excerpt: Beethoven's Symphony No. 1 in C major, movement II

The second movement of Symphony No. 1 in C major, Op. 21 by Ludwig van Beethoven (1770–1827) starts like a fugue, with a subject beginning C–F (dominant to tonic) played by second violins, and a tonal answer from violas and cellos on F–C (tonic to dominant). A further entry of the subject, in first violins doubled by woodwind at bar 12, forms part of a homophonic texture, with harmony entirely based on chords I and V⁷. So this is not to be a fugue after all, but a mostly light, dance-like movement (in sonata form). The two opening notes of the 'fugue' subject are however the source of much subtle humour later, not least as their interval is variously contracted (to a minor 3rd or even a minor 2nd) and expanded (up to a minor 7th), inverted and given different rhythmic emphases. Beethoven's ability to make a great deal out of tiny amounts of thematic material was one of the outstanding characteristics of his genius.

Related set works: Haydn's Symphony No. 26 in D minor, movement I (*NAM* 2) – symphony; Brahms' Piano Quintet in F minor, Op. 34, movement III (*NAM* 18) *and* Shostakovich's Prelude and Fugue in A, Op. 87, No. 7 (*NAM* 25) – fugal textures, for which see also Bach's Cantata No. 48, movements I–IV (*NAM* 28) – especially movement I, and Bach's Partita No. 4 in D, BWV 828 (*NAM* 21) – especially the Gigue.

(a)

There are 11 pitches and 11 note lengths to complete.

0	No work offered
1	1–2 pitches and/or note lengths correct
2	3–5 pitches and/or note lengths correct
3	6–8 pitches and/or note lengths correct
4	9–11 pitches and/or note lengths correct
5	12–14 pitches and note lengths correct
6	15–17 pitches and note lengths correct
7	18–20 pitches and note lengths correct
8	21–22 pitches and note lengths correct

> If you add the melody line in bars 36–38, consult a score of the music for the answer.

(b) (i)   Chord A: I/tonic (1); chord B: V⁷/dominant seventh (1)

    (ii) F major/tonic (1); imperfect (1). *Note*: this is not a plagal cadence in C, despite ending with chords of F and C major and having a B♮ (the briefest of auxiliary notes) in bar 24.

    (iii) Diminished seventh (1)

    (iv) A minor/mediant minor/relative minor of dominant (1)

    (v)   <u>Dominant</u> pedal (1)

(c) (i)   Imitation (1). Accept instead 'fugue' (as the writing has struck some writers as fugal in manner).

    (ii) Accept any year between 1780 and 1830 (1)

    (iii) B – Beethoven (1)

Question 2: Aural Awareness (2017)

Test 1

Excerpt: Handel's Concerto in F major, Op. 3, No. 4, movement II

Concerto Op. 3, No. 4 by George Frideric Handel (1685–1759) is classified sometimes as a concerto grosso, sometimes as an oboe concerto, but does not fall readily into any single category. The first movement is a purely orchestral French overture; the second has a part for oboe solo (although it is rarely independent of the first violins); the third employs two oboes, which largely double the violins. Handel's six concerti Op. 3 were published in London in 1734, although much of the music dates from well before this. Op. 3, No. 4, for example, was performed in 1716 at the King's Theatre, Haymarket, London as an 'orchestral concerto' between acts of the opera *Amadigi*.

Related set work: Corelli's Trio Sonata in D, Op. 3, No. 2, movement IV (*NAM* 15) – Baroque music for small ensemble.

(a)

There are 11 pitches and 11 note lengths to complete.

0	No work offered
1	1–3 pitches and/or note lengths correct
2	4–6 pitches and/or note lengths correct
3	7–9 pitches and/or note lengths correct
4	10–11 pitches and/or note lengths correct
5	12–14 pitches and note lengths correct
6	15–17 pitches and note lengths correct
7	18–20 pitches and note lengths correct
8	21–22 pitches and note lengths correct

(b) (i)   Bar 4: IV/subdominant (1); bar 36: VI/submediant (1)

 (ii)   Both are dominant pedals (in F major/tonic) (1); bars 9–12: inverted/bars 43–47: pedal in bass (1); bars 9–12: sustained note/bars 43–47: repeated notes and octave leaps (1). Max. 2.

 (iii) Bars 24–27: C major/dominant (1); bars 50–52: B♭ major/subdominant (1)

 (iv)   Suspension (1)

 (v)   Imperfect/Phrygian (1)

(c) (i)   Concerto grosso/orchestral concerto/oboe concerto (1)

 (ii)   B – Handel (1)

Test 2

Excerpt: Bach's Cantata No. 80 (*Ein' feste Burg*), movements VI and VII

As cantor to the Thomaskirche in Leipzig, Johann Sebastian Bach (1685–1750) was required to provide a cantata (a multi-sectional vocal/choral work with instrumental accompaniment) for each Sunday and festival day of the church year. His Cantata No. 80, *Ein' feste Burg*, was intended for the Reformation Festivals during the years 1727–1731, and drew on the Lutheran hymn associated above all with the German Protestant Reformation. This excerpt, however, consists of a recitative (a sort of musically heightened speech ['So take thy stand by Jesus' blood-spattered banner'] with continuo accompaniment) that merges with a more lyrical arioso marked by text-repetition ['Salvation now is sure']. The final section is a duet for tenor and alto ['Blessed is he who praises God whose words will sanctify him'], with obbligato parts for oboe da caccia and violin. For a further example of Bach's approach to this genre, see *NAM* 28.

Related set work: Gabrieli's *In ecclesiis* (*NAM* 27) – Baroque sacred music.

(a)

There are 10 pitches and 10 note lengths to complete.

0	No work offered
1	1–2 pitches and/or note lengths correct
2	3–4 pitches and/or note lengths correct
3	5–7 pitches and/or note lengths correct
4	8–10 pitches and/or note lengths correct
5	11–13 pitches and note lengths correct
6	14–16 pitches and note lengths correct
7	17–18 pitches and note lengths correct
8	19–20 pitches and note lengths correct

(b) (i) Bars 9–10: A major (1). Accept instead relative major of dominant (of the recitative's opening and closing B minor) *or* dominant (of the arioso's closing D major). Bars 22–26: D major/dominant (of the duet's opening G major) (1). Accept instead relative major (of the recitative's opening B minor).

(ii) V⁷d/dominant 7th in third inversion (1)

(iii) Diminished 7th (1)

(iv) Bars 15–16: interrupted (1); end: perfect (1)

(v) Bar 21: suspension (with ornamental resolution) (1); bar 35: échappée (1)

(c) (i) Cantata/oratorio (1)

(ii) A – Bach (1)

Test 3

Excerpt: Beethoven's Piano Sonata in D, Op. 10, No. 3, movement II

Beethoven's Sonata Op. 10, No. 3 was composed in 1797, not long before the Septet. It forms a fascinating contrast with the latter, indicating that some of Beethoven's most deeply felt earlier works were reserved for the piano. Notice how the melody line is intensified by appoggiaturas, and how the harmonic tension is kept high by the plentiful use of diminished 7th and augmented 6th chords. Keep listening to this excerpt even after you have completed the test, perhaps with a score, to help you become increasingly familiar with the characteristic sounds of these two important types of chromatic chord.

Related set works: Beethoven's Septet in E♭, Op. 20, movement I (*NAM* 17) – music by Beethoven *and* chamber music of the Classical period; Mozart's Piano Sonata in B♭, K. 333, movement I (*NAM* 22) – the piano sonata in the Classical period.

(a)

Accept crotchet E in place of quaver E, quaver rest in second bar above, and/or crotchet C in place of quaver C, quaver rest.

There are 9 pitches and 9 note lengths to complete.

0	No work offered
1	1–2 pitches and/or note lengths correct
2	3–4 pitches and/or note lengths correct
3	5–6 pitches and/or note lengths correct
4	7–9 pitches and/or note lengths correct
5	10–12 pitches and note lengths correct
6	13–14 pitches and note lengths correct
7	15–16 pitches and note lengths correct
8	17–18 pitches and note lengths correct

(b) (i) G minor/subdominant (minor) (1)

    (ii) C major/dominant (major) of relative major/relative major of dominant (minor) (1)

    (iii) A minor/dominant (minor) (1); perfect (1)

    (iv) Bar 8: Ic/second inversion of tonic (in D minor/tonic) (1); bar 17: augmented 6th (1)

    (v) Diminished 7th (1)

    (vi) Appoggiatura (1)

(c) (i) Second/slow (1)

    (ii) A – Beethoven (1)

Test 4

Excerpt: 'See, I obey' from Purcell's *The Fairy Queen*

Henry Purcell (1659–1695) was by far the most outstanding English-born composer of the Baroque period. He wrote a good deal of sacred music for the church, but his reputation rests above all on music for the royal court and the theatre. *The Fairy Queen*, first performed at the Queen's Theatre in 1692, is sometimes described as a 'semi-opera'. This is a form partly descended from the courtly 17th-century masque but also influenced by contemporary French opera. Accordingly, and unlike the 'full' opera *Dido and Aeneas*, it does not have music continuously, but combines song, dance and a spoken play (an anonymous adaptation of Shakespeare's *A Midsummer Night's Dream*). The excerpt here is sung by Hymen, the god of marriage, on being summoned to join the festivities.

Related set works: Gabrieli's *In ecclesiis* (*NAM* 27) – 17th-century Baroque vocal music; Corelli's Trio Sonata in D, Op. 3, No. 2, movement IV (*NAM* 15) – late 17th-century music.

(a)

There are 11 pitches and 11 note lengths to complete.

0	No work offered
1	1–3 pitches and/or note lengths correct
2	4–6 pitches and/or note lengths correct
3	7–9 pitches and/or note lengths correct
4	10–11 pitches and/or note lengths correct
5	12–14 pitches and note lengths correct
6	15–17 pitches and note lengths correct
7	18–20 pitches and note lengths correct
8	21–22 pitches and note lengths correct

(b) (i) Bar 14: A minor (1), perfect (1); bars 24–25: E minor (1); imperfect/Phrygian (1)

(ii) G major (1)

(iii) Suspension (1)

(iv) Dominant pedal (1)

(c) (i) Accept any of the following: secular/stage-work/opera/semi-opera/masque/ode/cantata (1)

(ii) D – Purcell (1)

(iii) C – 1692 (1)

Section B: Music in Context

For Section B and C questions, it is impossible to give a totally comprehensive mark scheme that lists all the possible points that you might make. Instead we have provided for each question what examiners call 'indicative content' – that is, a list of the main relevant points.

In every Section B answer you write, you should illustrate the points made with detailed references to the music under discussion, wherever appropriate. Such references will gain you additional credit. To see how this works, consult Edexcel's indicative content in the Sample Assessment Materials for Unit 6. For example, nine or more relevant points with only limited illustration would be awarded nine or ten marks out of this 13-mark maximum.

Applied Music 2015: Gabrieli

➤ 'Early' instruments required, e.g. cornett, early violin (close in range to modern viola), trombones
➤ Harmony involves:
  ➤ Mainly root positions and first inversions
  ➤ Cadences (Phrygian and plagal as well as perfect)
  ➤ Suspensions, notably 4–3 and 7–6
  ➤ Tierce de Picardie.

> These features are not exclusive to music such as Gabrieli's, but are typical of it and therefore it is appropriate to refer to them.

➤ Tonality is typical of Renaissance era:
  ➤ Modal (Dorian on G)
  ➤ Cadences on most degrees of the mode, resulting in considerable tonal variety.

Applied Music 2016: ET: Flying Theme

Rhythm
➤ Motor rhythms in introduction plus ostinato
➤ Repeated quavers in accompaniment to main theme.

Melody
➤ Sweeping theme with wide intervals (5th, 7th, octave) and common-chord framework
➤ Major mode, except for Lydian inflections (sharpened fourths) at bar 75 onwards.

Orchestration
➤ Exhilaration of experience emphasised by orchestration (bells, theme doubled across several octaves).

Applied Music 2017: Stravinsky

➤ Based directly on a solo cello sonata by 18th-century composer Pergolesi
➤ Rather than pastiche or arrangement, it is what Stravinsky referred to as 'recomposition'
➤ Recomposition achieved through:
  ➤ Novel instrumentation and instrumental techniques, e.g. transfer of cello part to double bass, often in a high register; prominent solo trombone, with glissandi
  ➤ Unusual textures, e.g. heterophony
  ➤ Freer handling of dissonance than in 18th-century music
  ➤ Modified perfect cadences
  ➤ Unexpected stresses/syncopation, emphasised by 'du talon' performance
  ➤ Interpolation of extra bars.

Section C: Continuity and Change in Instrumental Music

In every Section C answer you write, you should illustrate the points made with detailed references to the music under discussion, wherever appropriate. Such reference will gain you additional credit. To see how this works, consult Edexcel's indicative content in the Sample Assessment Materials for Unit 6. For example, 18 or more relevant, well-illustrated points will secure you a mark in the outstanding category (i.e. 32–36 marks), providing of course that you write in continuous prose and that your work is well organised, with a convincing style of writing and few errors in spelling or grammar. In contrast, an essay with a similar number of relevant points without extensive illustration would gain you a mark of between 24 and 27 out of the 30-mark maximum.

Instrumental Music 2015

Melody

Beethoven:
➤ Periodic phrasing
➤ Frequent scalic lines
➤ Ornamentation
➤ Use of sequence.

Armstrong:
➤ Improvisation
➤ Chromaticism
➤ Wide range overall
➤ Repetition.

Tippett:
➤ Motivic
➤ Varying phrase lengths
➤ Various intervallic patterns, ranging from stepwise to more angular shapes
➤ Modality
➤ Inversion
➤ Sequence
➤ Ornamentation.

Harmony

Beethoven:
➤ Functional
➤ Perfect and imperfect cadences
➤ Varying harmonic rhythm
➤ Includes root, 1st and 2nd inversions, dominant 7ths and augmented 6ths.

Armstrong:
➤ Twelve-bar blues harmonic progression
➤ Augmented triad at bar 6
➤ Substitution chords
➤ Decorated plagal cadence at close, consisting of $A\flat m^7 - E\flat^6$.

Tippett:
➤ Rarely chordal textures
➤ Occasional cadences, including perfect and modal
➤ Final chord without a third
➤ Augmented triad, e.g. bar 124.

Instrumental Music 2016

Instrumentation

Haydn:
➤ Scored for small classical orchestra that still incorporates harpsichord.

Brahms:
➤ Romantic sound evident in use of piano and solo strings, all requiring considerable performance skill.

Ellington:
➤ Typical of a transitional late-1920s style of jazz involving an ensemble larger than that found in earlier, more traditional jazz
➤ Some using 'jungle' style techniques.

Texture

Haydn:
➤ Chiefly homophonic (credit for details)
➤ First subject has a 'lean' two-part texture
➤ Pedals.

Brahms:
➤ Wide range of textures including:
  ➤ Octaves
  ➤ Imitation
  ➤ Fugato
  ➤ Melody-dominated homophony
  ➤ Homorhythm
  ➤ Pedals.

Ellington:
➤ Mainly melody-dominated homophony with improvised melodies
➤ Stride textures in piano solo.

Instrumental Music 2017

Melody

Shostakovich:
➤ Often the most prominent part of the texture, thrown into relief by drones
➤ With prominence given to the DSCH motif
➤ Melodies are often chromatic
➤ Appoggiaturas
➤ Much conjunct movement
➤ Narrow-range motifs (including the DSCH figure)
➤ Repetition of motifs
➤ Use of sequence.

Cage:
➤ The usual features of melody are difficult to discern because of preparation/distortion of pitch, etc.
➤ On paper, some apparently chromatic and pentatonic elements
➤ Angular lines.

Corelli:
➤ Combination of conjunct movement with broken-chord figures
➤ Some inversion of main motif
➤ Fragmentation of main motif
➤ Sequence.

Rhythm

Shostakovich:
➤ Generally slow-moving in simple quadruple time
➤ Some long-held drones
➤ Some dotted-crotchet quaver rhythms.

Cage:
➤ Fractal/micro-macrocosmic scheme in which small-scale rhythmic durations determine the overall proportions of the structure
➤ Sonata I uses seven <u>crotchet units</u> in sets of 4–1–3 (repeated); 4–2 (repeated)
➤ These are the rhythmic cells of bars 1–7, amounting to 28 crotchets
➤ Sonata II: $1\frac{1}{2} + 1\frac{1}{2} + 2\frac{3}{8} + 2\frac{3}{8}$ applied to 31 crotchets
➤ Sonata III: $1 + 1 + 3\frac{1}{4} + 3\frac{1}{4}$ applied to 34 crotchets
➤ At surface level, the Sonatas are marked by:
  ➤ Off-beat effects
  ➤ Triplets
  ➤ Other irregular note groupings
  ➤ Rhythmic displacements of short patterns.
➤ III makes use of a more regular pulse
➤ Frequent changes of time signature.

Corelli:
➤ Gigue-like compound duple, involving groups of quavers and semiquavers
➤ Hemiola.

Track information by question

Question 1: Comparison (2015)

Test 1: tracks 1-2

Vivaldi: Concerto in D minor, Op. 3, No. 11, movements II and III

The English Concert, Pinnock (cond.)

Vivaldi: L'estro armonico (Op. 3), 6 flute concertos (Op. 10) (DG Archiv 477 5421)

CD2 track 5, 0:00-0:57; CD2 track 6, 0:00-0:52

Test 2: tracks 3-4

Beethoven: *Fidelio*, Act 1, No. 4 ('Hat man nicht auch Gold beineben') and No. 7 ('Ha! Welch' ein Augenblick!')

London Symphony Orchestra, Davis (cond.)

Beethoven: Fidelio (LSO 0593)

Track 8, 0:00-1:01; track 13, 0:00-1:03

Test 3: tracks 5-6

Stravinsky: Symphony in C, movements I and IV

Philharmonia Orchestra, Craft (cond.)

Stravinsky: Symphony in C, Symphony in Three Movements, Octet for Winds, Dumbarton Oaks Concerto (Naxos 8.557507)

Track 7, 0:00-0:54; track 10, 0:00-1:18

Test 4: tracks 7-8

Morehouse and Trumbauer: *Three Blind Mice* and *Krazy Kat*

Bix Beiderbecke: *Jazz Masters: Bix Beiderbecke* (EMI CDMFP 6297)

Track 13, 0:00-1:07; track 14, 0:00-1:03

Question 1: Comparison (2016)

Test 1: tracks 9-10

Handel: *Let God Arise*, HWV 256b, movements III and IV

Chapel Royal Choir, Gant (cond.)

Handel: Music for the Chapel Royal (Naxos 8.557935)

Track 3, 0:00-1:11; track 4, 0:00-1:06

Test 2: track 11

Schubert: Symphony No. 5, movement III

New York Chamber Orchestra, Schwarz (cond.)

Schubert: Musically Speaking – Symphony No. 5, 'Unfinished' Symphony No. 8, German Dances (Eroica Classical)

Track 4, 0:00-1:11

Test 2: track 12

Schubert: Symphony No. 9 (the 'Great C major'), movement III

Orchestre de l'Opéra de Lyon, Gardiner (cond.)

Schubert: Symphonies Nos. 8-9 (Erato)

Track 3, 0:00-1:07

Test 3: tracks 13-14

Bernstein: *West Side Story*, Act 1, No. 5 ('Maria'), and Act 2, No. 15 ('A Boy Like That')

National Symphony Orchestra, Edwards (cond.)

West Side Story (1993 Leicester Haymarket Theatre)(TER 1197)

CD1 track 10, 0:00-1:33; CD2 track 10, 0:00-1:12

Test 4: tracks 15-16

Debussy: 'Pagodes' from *Estampes*, and 'Jimbo's Lullaby' from *Children's Corner*

Pascal Rogé: *Debussy: Children's Corner, Estampes, Suite Bergamasque* (ONYX 4018)

Track 1, 0:00-1:21; track 5, 0:00-1:22

Question 1: Comparison (2017)

Test 1: tracks 17–18

Shostakovich: Symphony No. 9, Op. 70, movements I and IV

Belgian Radio and Television Philharmonic Orchestra, Rahbari (cond.)

Shostakovich: Symphony No. 5 / Symphony No. 9 (Naxos 8.550427)

Track 5, 0:00–1:03; track 8, 0:00–1:14

Test 2: tracks 19–20

Monteverdi: *Vespers*, 'Deposuit potentes' and 'Suscepit Israel' from the Magnificat

Scholars Baroque Ensemble

Monteverdi: Vespers of the Blessed Virgin (Naxos, 8.550662–63)

CD2 track 9, 0:00–1:33; CD2 track 11, complete

Test 3: tracks 21–22

Walton: *Henry V*, 'Prologue' and 'Epilogue'

BBC Singers, Trinity Boys Choir, BBC Symphony Orchestra, Leonard Slatkin (cond.)

William Walton: Henry V (BBC MM215)

Track 1, 0:00–1:31; track 10, 4:32–5:38

Test 4: track 23

Schubert: String Quartet in D minor ('Death and the Maiden'), movement IV

Endellion String Quartet

Schubert: Quartet in D minor / Quartet in A minor (BBC MM55)

Track 4, 0:00–0:50

Test 4: track 24

Schubert: Octet in F major, movement VI

Michael Collins (clarinet) and others

Schubert: Octet (BBC MM86)

Track 6, 0:00–1:20

Question 2: Aural Awareness (2015)

Test 1: track 25

Haydn: Symphony No. 101 in D, movement I

Royal Philharmonic Orchestra, Glover (cond.)

Haydn: Symphony No. 101 (The Clock), Symphony No. 103 (Drum Roll) (Membran 222840)

Track 1, 0:00-2:31

Test 2: track 26

Mozart: Piano Concerto No. 23 in A, K. 488, movement II

The Academy of St Martin in the Fields, Marriner (cond.), Brendel

Mozart: Piano Concertos Nos. 15, 21 and 23 (Decca)

Track 8, 0:00-2:17

Test 3: track 27

Weber: 'Kommt ein schlanker Bursch gegangen' from *Der Freischütz*

Berliner Philharmoniker, Keilberth (cond.)

Weber: Der Freischütz (EMI Classics 2088212)

Track 16, 0:00-2:19

Test 4: track 28

Vivaldi: 'Domine Deus, Agnus Dei' from *Gloria*

Academy of St Martin in the Fields, Kings's College Choir, Willcocks (cond.), Baker

Haydn: Nelson Mass, Vivaldi: Gloria in D, Handel: Zadok the Priest (Decca 4586232)

Track 19, 0:00-2:27

Question 2: Aural Awareness (2016)

Test 1: track 29

Bach: Fugue from Toccata and Fugue in F, BWV 540

Walter Kraft: *Bach: Complete Organ Music* (Musical Concepts MC 191)

CD5 track 2, 0:00-2:23

Test 2: track 30

Brahms: 'An die Nachtigall' from *Vier Lieder*, Op. 46

Bernarda Fink, Roger Vignoles: *Brahms: Lieder* (Harmonia Mundi HMC 901926)

Track 8, 0:00-2:47

Test 3: track 31

Bach: 'Erbarme dich, mein Gott' from *St Matthew Passion*

Hungarian State Symphony Orchestra, Hungarian Festival Choir, Oberfrank (cond.)

Bach: Favourite Arias and Choruses (Naxos 8.553257)

Track 8, 0:00-2:19

Test 4: track 32

Beethoven: Symphony No. 1 in C major, movement II

Berliner Staatskapelle, Barenboim (cond.)

Beethoven: Symphonies Nos. 1-2 (Teldec 8573-83085-9)

Track 2, 0:00-2:15

Question 2: Aural Awareness (2017)

Test 1: track 33

Handel: Concerto in F major, Op. 3, No. 4, movement II

Northern Sinfonia, Creswick (cond.)

Handel: Concerti Grossi Op. 3, Nos. 1–6 (Naxos 8.553457)

Track 14, complete

Test 2: track 34

Bach: Cantata No. 80, movements VI and VII

Nemeth (alto), Mukk (tenor), Hungarian Radio Chorus, Failoni Chamber Orchestra Budapest, Antál (cond.)

J. S. Bach: Cantatas, BWV 80 and 147 (Naxos 8.550642)

Track 6, complete; track 7, 0:00–1:01

Test 3: track 35

Beethoven: Piano Sonata in D, Op. 10, No. 3, movement II

Jenö Jandó

Beethoven: Piano Sonatas, Vol. 5 (Naxos 8.550161)

Track 8, 0:00–2:43

Test 4: track 36

Purcell: *The Fairy Queen*, 'See, I obey'

Owen Brannigan, English Chamber Orchestra

Purcell: The Fairy Queen / Dido and Aeneas (Decca 4685612)

CD2 track 4, complete

Glossary

This glossary is not comprehensive: it refers to terms as used in this volume. For definitions of any common terms relating to tonality and harmony not included here, see the AS Harmony Workbook and/or the A2 Harmony Workbook (Rhinegold Education, 2008). More information on types of dissonance and types of chord is also available in these books. For instruments and fuller definitions of other terms and expressions, consult the Dictionary of Music in Sound (Rhinegold Education, 2002).

Acciaccatura. A very short ornamental note played before a principal melodic note, written or printed as ♪.

Accidental. A symbol that changes the pitch of a note, usually by a semitone.

Aeolian mode. A scale that uses the following pattern of tones (T) and semitones (s): T–s–T–T–s–T–T. When starting on A, it consists of all the white notes within one octave on a keyboard.

Affekt. German word meaning 'emotion' or 'mood'. Applied to a particular emotion or mood that lasts throughout a Baroque piece of music. Baroque composers (unlike those of the Classical period and later) often preferred to maintain a single *Affekt* throughout a movement rather than introduce marked changes of mood.

Afro-Cuban jazz. A style of jazz that combines **bebop** and Cuban elements, often involving polyrhythm.

Anthem. A type of church music for choir, often accompanied by organ, and occasionally by larger forces. An anthem usually has English words (often from the Bible). In Church of England services, for which Handel wrote when he was in England, there are special places for anthems in the services of Morning and Evening Prayer (also known as Mattins and Evensong). *See also* **Verse anthem.**

Anticipation. A melody note (frequently the tonic of the key in the highest part) sounded slightly before the chord to which it belongs, thereby creating a dissonance with the previous chord.

Antiphony. Performance by different singers/instrumentalists in alternation. Often – but not always – the different groups perform similar material.

Appoggiatura. A non-chord note that sounds on the beat and then resolves by step (up or down a semitone or tone) to the main chord note. The dissonant note is not 'prepared' as a suspension is. Although appoggiaturas are normally approached by leap, accented passing notes that are particularly long and/or prominent are often described as appoggiaturas, even though they are approached by step. Sometimes an appoggiatura, especially in music of the Classical period, is indicated by a note in small type, followed by its resolution printed at normal size.

Aria. A song (usually from an opera, oratorio or cantata) for solo voice, plus accompaniment for orchestra or, sometimes in Baroque times, for smaller forces, even just continuo. An aria often provides a character in an opera with the opportunity to reflect at length on their emotional state.

Arioso. A section or piece that is part way between an **aria** and a **recitative** in the manner of text-setting and level of musical interest.

Atonal. Atonal music avoids keys or modes; that is, no pitch stands out consistently in the way the tonic does in tonal music.

Augmentation. The lengthening of the rhythmic values of a previously-heard melody (e.g. where ♩♪♪ has become ♩♩♩).

Augmented interval. An interval that is one semitone wider than a major or perfect interval with the same number. For example, an augmented 5th (e.g. G–D♯) is one semitone wider than a perfect 5th (G–D); an augmented 4th (e.g. F–B) is one semitone wider than a perfect 4th (F–B♭).

Augmented 6th chord. A chromatic chord which in root position spans the interval of an augmented 6th, e.g. A♭–F♯. The chord also includes the major 3rd above the root (and sometimes also the perfect 5th or augmented 4th).

Auxiliary note. A non-chord note that occurs between, and is a tone or semitone above or below, two harmony notes of the same pitch.

Ballad. Originally a type of narrative verse, particularly from the British Isles, set in strophic fashion with the same music for each stanza. (Nowadays can just mean a love song.)

Baritone. A type of male voice higher than a bass and lower than a tenor.

Bebop. A style of jazz that developed in the 1940s from swing. More complex and less easy to dance to, it was characterised by improvisation, fast tempos, irregular phrase lengths and a greater emphasis on the rhythm section.

Cadence. A pair of chords signifying the end of a phrase in tonal music. Cadences are of several types, of which perfect and imperfect are by far the most common. *See also* **Imperfect cadence, Interrupted cadence, Perfect cadence** and **Phrygian cadence.**

Cadenza. A showy passage for a soloist, usually without accompaniment: sometimes long and most commonly found towards the end of the first movement of a concerto. Many 18th-century cadenzas sat between chords Ic and V in a perfect cadence (which is how the name 'cadenza' – Italian for 'cadence' – came to be applied). In the 18th century cadenzas were usually improvised, ending with a prolonged trill to provide a signal to the orchestra to re-enter.

Call and response. Originally signified a phrase sung by one person and answered by a different phrase sung by others. It is sometimes used as a synonym for antiphony. *See also* **Antiphony**.

Canon. A strict form of imitation, often lasting for a substantial passage or entire piece, where the second part is an exact (or almost exact) copy of the first, even if at a different pitch.

Cantata. Usually a work for voice(s) and instruments in several movements. A cantata is generally shorter than an oratorio, sometimes without chorus, and can be sacred or secular. (In the early 17th century the term cantata (Italian for 'sung') could be applied to more or less any sung piece.) *See also* **Oratorio**.

Chorale. A German hymn of the kind sung in the Lutheran (Protestant) church in the time of J. S. Bach. The word 'chorale' can refer to the words only, or the associated melody only, or to the whole hymn. Chorale melodies are largely stepwise (or conjunct): their harmonisation has long featured in advanced music courses.

Chordal. A form of homophony in which all the parts either move together in the same rhythm or have very limited independent rhythmic movement. The term **homorhythmic** (literally 'same rhythm') is sometimes used instead.

Chromatic. A chromatic note is one that does not belong to the scale of the key currently in use. For example, in D major the notes G♯ and C♮ are chromatic. The tonality of a passage containing many chromatic notes may be described as chromatic.

Circle of 5ths. Harmonic progression in which the roots of the chords move by descending 5ths (and/or ascending 4ths), e.g. B–E–A–D–G–C, etc.

Compound time. A metre in which the main beat is subdivided into three equal portions. Opposite of **Simple time**.

Concertato. Concertato style, used mainly in the first half of the 17th century, involved contrasts between different groups of performers, usually both vocal and instrumental.

Concertino. The group of soloists in a Baroque concerto grosso – most commonly two violins and a cello (as in Corelli's Op. 6 concertos).

Concerto. Most commonly, a work for a soloist with orchestra. In many concertos the solo instrument is a piano or violin. Occasionally there may be two soloists (a double concerto) or even three (a triple concerto). (In the 17th century the term was used more widely, and was applied originally to a work in which voices and instruments, with more or less independent parts, collaborated in a manner that was new at the time.) *See also* **Concerto grosso**.

Concerto grosso. A type of concerto, most common in the late Baroque period, in which three (or occasionally more) soloists, known as the Concertino, are contrasted with the sound of a larger group of mainly string instruments, know as the Ripieno.

Conjunct. Melodic movement by step rather than by leap. Opposite of **disjunct**.

Continuo. Short for 'basso continuo' (Italian for 'continuous bass'), and used chiefly in Baroque music. Refers to an instrumental bassline (most commonly played by cello(s), sometimes with bass(es)), together with an improvised accompaniment on keyboard or lute, which supplies full harmony that might otherwise be lacking.

Contrapuntal. Adjective to describe music that uses **counterpoint**. Counterpoint involves two or more melodic lines (usually rhythmically contrasted), each significant in itself, which are played or sung together – in contrast to **homophony**, in which one part has the melody and the other parts accompany. The term 'polyphonic' is often used as a synonym for contrapuntal.

Counterpoint. *See* **Contrapuntal**.

Countertenor. A type of adult male voice higher than a tenor, which often involves use of a special high vocal register known as falsetto. The term 'male alto' is sometimes employed for those countertenors who use the falsetto register.

Cross-rhythm. The use of two or more very different rhythms simultaneously in different parts. One rhythm may imply one metre (or time signature), while another implies a different one.

Cyclic. Cyclic treatment involves the use of the same thematic material in two or more movements (usually of a sonata or symphony).

Dialogue. When two or more instruments or voices have a musical 'conversation', with the individual parts responding to one another.

Diatonic. Using notes that belong to the current key. A diatonic note is one that belongs to the scale of the key currently in use. For example, in D major the notes D, E and F♯ are diatonic.

Diminished 7th. A dissonant four-note chord made up of super-imposed minor 3rds (for example C♯–E–G–B♭).

Disjunct. Melodic movement by leap rather than by step. Opposite of **conjunct**.

Dissonance. Any note not a major or minor 3rd or 6th, perfect 5th, unison or perfect octave above the lowest part sounding is strictly a dissonance. Triads in root position or in first inversion are therefore the only chords that have no dissonance. (Even the 4th above the bass in a second inversion counts as dissonant.) Some dissonances, particularly suspensions and appoggiaturas, add harmonic tension and can help make the music more expressive; others, notably passing and auxiliary notes, provide rhythmic and melodic decoration.

Divertimento. A piece (most commonly from the 18th century) whose style is partly or wholly light and intended to 'divert' or 'amuse' listeners, perhaps at a social function. A divertimento is normally in several movements, with at least one in a dance (particularly minuet) style.

Dixieland. A name given to traditional jazz, particularly when played by white musicians in the period between about 1917 and 1930, although also used for later revivals of the style. It lacked some of the feeling for swung rhythms and blues inflections characteristic of early black jazz, but helped to extend the melodic and harmonic vocabulary of jazz.

Dominant 7th. A dissonant four-note chord built on the dominant note of the scale. It includes the dominant triad plus a minor 7th above the root.

Dorian mode. A scale that uses the following pattern of tones (T) and semitones (s): T–s–T–T–T–s–T. When starting on D, it consists of all the white notes within one octave on a keyboard.

Drone. A sustained note (or sometimes sustained tonic and dominant notes) against which other parts play or sing melodies, especially in music that shows some folk influence. There is not necessarily any dissonance as there is with a **pedal**.

Du talon. Direction to a string player to use the part of the bow hair nearest to the heel (near where the player holds the bow), producing a stronger, rougher attack.

Échappée. An échappée (or 'escape note') leaves a harmony note by step (usually upwards) and then leaps in the opposite direction (usually by a 3rd) to a new harmony note.

Expressionism. One of the most important musical movements of the 20th century, led by the composers Schoenberg, Berg and Webern. As the name suggests, it applies to music in which a composer's inner turmoil is reflected in unsettled, chaotic music.

False relation. The occurrence of the ordinary and chromatically altered versions of the same note (such as F♯ and F♮) in two different parts at the same time, or in close proximity.

Free jazz. Avant-garde jazz of the 1960s, with a loose approach to tonality, chord sequences and structure.

Fugal. *See* **Fugue.**

Fugato. A passage in fugal style which forms part of a larger piece of music.

Fugue. A type of piece in which a theme called a 'subject' is treated in imitation by all the parts (usually with short passages called 'episodes' from which it is absent, for relief and contrast). The adjective is **fugal** (for instance, 'in fugal style' means 'in the style of a fugue').

Functional harmony. A type of harmony that has the *function* of defining a major or minor key, in particular through chords on the tonic and dominant (I and V$^{(7)}$), with special emphasis on perfect cadences (V$^{(7)}$–I).

Gamelan. An ensemble from Indonesia (usually Bali or Java) consisting largely of tuned percussion.

Genre. A type of music. Genres include the sonata, the string quartet and the symphony.

Glissando. A slide between two notes.

Gongan. In **gamelan** music, a rhythmic unit concluded by the sounding of the Gong.

Gymel. In English vocal music of the late 15th and early 16th centuries, the temporary division of a single voice part (especially the treble part) into two to provide additional fullness or brightness of texture.

Harmonic rhythm. The rate at which harmony changes in a piece.

Harmonics. A technique of lightly touching a string on a string instrument to produce an artificial high sound (sometimes rather flute-like in sound).

Hemiola. The articulation of two units of triple time (strong–weak–weak, strong–weak–weak) as three units of duple time (strong–weak, strong–weak, strong–weak).

Heterophony. A texture in which a melody is performed simultaneously with one or more rhythmically and/or melodically varied versions of itself.

Homophony. A texture in which one part has a melody and the other parts accompany, in contrast to **contrapuntal** writing, where each part has independent melodic and rhythmic interest.

Imitation. Where a melodic idea in one part is immediately repeated in another part (exactly or inexactly), at the same or a different pitch, while the first part continues. The adjective is 'imitative'.

Imperfect cadence. An open-ended or inconclusive cadence ending with the dominant chord (V). The preceding chord is usually I, ii or IV.

Impressionism. A compositional movement that began in

France in the late 19th century and continued into the 20th, and was in some respects similar to the art movement of the same name. Important characteristics of impressionist music include heightened attention to timbre, colour and atmosphere, non-functional harmony and tonality and fluid metre.

Improvisation. The process of spontaneously creating new music, often basing this on existing musical material (such as a chord pattern) – in effect, it means performing music as you compose it. Improvisation is very common in jazz.

Instrumentation. The choice of instruments for a piece of music. (The expression 'instrumental forces' is sometimes used instead.)

Interrupted cadence. A cadence intended to create surprise or suspense, perhaps by delaying the arrival of a final perfect or plagal cadence. Usually an interrupted cadence consists of chord V followed by chord VI.

Inversion. When a chord has a note other than the root in the lowest part, it is an inversion. In a first-inversion chord the 3rd of the chord is the lowest part, and in a second-inversion chord the 5th. For example, a triad of F major in first inversion is A–C–F, and in second inversion is C–F–A.

Ionian mode. A scale that uses the following pattern of tones (T) and semitones (s): T–T–s–T–T–T–s. When starting on C, it consists of all the white notes within one octave on a keyboard.

Isorhythmic. Using a repeating rhythmic pattern in conjunction with the repetition of a pre-existing melody or cantus firmus, the rhythmic pattern and melodic repetition being 'out of phase'.

Jungle. A style of jazz developed by Duke Ellington in the 1920s, characterised especially by dark textures and growling brass effects.

Keteg. In **gamelan** music, individual rhythmic cells, the equivalent of bars, which together form the **gongan**.

Lied. German for song, but used in English to refer specifically to 19th-century settings of German poetry for an accompanied solo voice.

Lombardic rhythm. A 'reversed' dotted rhythm, with the shorter note first, e.g. semiquaver–dotted quaver. The term 'Scotch snap' is sometimes used instead.

Lydian mode/inflections. The Lydian mode is a scale that uses the following pattern of tones (T) and semitones (s): T–T–T–s–T–T–s. When starting on F, it consists of all the white notes within one octave on a keyboard. We speak of Lydian 'inflections' when music in F major has occasional B♮(s) in a manner characteristic of the Lydian mode.

Magnificat. The words of the Virgin Mary before the birth of Jesus (from the gospel of Luke, chapter 1), widely sung in church services, including the Church of England service of Evening Prayer or Evensong. 'Magnificat' is the first word of the Latin version of this song.

Mass. The Mass is the principal act of worship of the Roman Catholic Church; it corresponds in some ways with services of Holy Communion in other churches. The word 'mass' (often, as here, with a lower-case 'm') can also refer to a musical setting of certain texts from the Mass (for example, Gloria in excelsis and Sanctus).

Masque. Form of English court entertainment from the 17th and early 18th centuries – staged, with singing, instrumental music and dancing.

Melisma. In vocal music, a group of notes on a single syllable, often for expressive purposes or word-painting.

Melody-dominated homophony. As with 'ordinary' homophony, a texture in which one part has a melody and the other parts accompany. With melody-dominated homophony, however, the melody stands apart from the accompaniment particularly clearly and strongly.

Metre. Concerns the identity, grouping and subdivision of beats, as indicated by a time signature. E.g. the time signature ¾ indicates a simple triple metre, in which each bar consists of three crochet beats, any of which can be divided into two quavers. In contrast, ⅜ is a compound triple metre, in which each bar consists of three dotted-crotchet beats, any of which can be divided into three quavers.

Minuet. A dance in simple triple metre of French origin. 17th- and 18th-century composers often included pieces entitled minuet in suites and symphonies, but for listening to, not for dancing. A minuet was generally played through twice, with, in between, a 'trio' (another minuet in all but name). Most minuets were graceful and not very fast. *See also* **Scherzo.**

Modal. A term often used to refer to music based on a mode rather than on major and minor keys.

Modulation. A change of key, or the process of changing key.

Monophony. Music consisting only of a single melodic line. The adjective is 'monophonic'.

Mordent. A quick ornament, denoted by a conventional sign. There is movement from the main (printed or written) note to the note above (upper mordent) or below (lower mordent) and back again.

Motet. A type of church music for choir, sometimes accompanied by organ, and occasionally by larger forces. A motet often has Latin words (commonly from the Bible), and is particularly but not exclusively associated with Roman Catholic services.

Motif. A short but distinctive musical idea that is developed in various ways in order to create a longer passage of music. The adjective is 'motivic' (e.g. 'motivic development' means 'development of a motif').

Neapolitan 6th. A chromatic chord (often in a minor key) consisting of the first inversion of the major chord formed on the flattened supertonic, i.e. the flattened second degree of the scale (in D minor for example, the Neapolitan 6th has the notes G–B♭–E♭).

Neoclassical. A term used for music in which the composer revives elements from an earlier style (not necessarily a Classical one). These elements normally exist alongside more up-to-date ones – mere copying of an old style is 'pastiche'.

Obbligato. A prominent (and essential – 'obligatory') instrumental part in Baroque music, often in an aria, in addition to the vocal part and continuo.

Opera. A large-scale dramatic work for singers and instrumentalists. In most cases the whole text is sung, so that an opera is very different from a play with incidental music. An opera differs from a musical too (for example, the music is not generally popular in idiom).

Oratorio. A large-scale work on a religious subject for solo voice(s), chorus and instruments in a number of movements. *See also* **Cantata**.

Ornamentation. Addition of melodic decoration, often through the use of conventional forms of ornamentation such as **trills** and **mordents**.

Ostinato. A repeating melodic, harmonic or rhythmic motif, heard continuously throughout part or the whole of a piece.

Passing note. A non-harmony note approached and quitted by step in the same direction, often filling in a melodic gap of a 3rd (e.g. A between G and B, where both G and B are harmony notes).

Passion. A musical setting of the story of the sufferings and death on the cross of Jesus Christ as told in the New Testament of the Bible. An oratorio Passion is one which, like Bach's St Matthew, includes non-biblical words in addition to those of the biblical narrative.

Pedal. A sustained or repeated note, usually in a low register, over which changing harmonies occur. A pedal on the fifth note of the scale (a dominant pedal) tends to create a sense of expectation in advance of a perfect cadence; a pedal on the keynote (a tonic pedal) can create a feeling of repose.

Perfect cadence. A cadence ending with the tonic chord (I), preceded by the dominant (V or V⁷) – appropriate where some degree of finality is required.

Pelog. In **gamelan** music, a seven-note scale. Often, as in *Baris Melampahan*, only five notes from such a scale are actually used.

Pentatonic. A scale made up of five notes, most frequently the first, second, third, fifth and sixth degrees of a major scale (for example, the major pentatonic scale of C is C–D–E–G–A).

Periodic phrasing. Phrases of regular length (two- and four-bar phrases, and multiples thereof) are deliberately combined to form balanced larger units, sometimes with a clear sense of 'question and answer' or 'antecedent and consequent'. Particularly found in Classical-period music.

Phrygian cadence. A type of imperfect cadence, in which the dominant chord (V) is preceded by the first inversion of the subdominant (IVb). It is used chiefly in minor keys, and particularly in Baroque music.

Pivot chord. A chord that links together two different keys in a modulation and is common to both of them. For example, the chord of D minor is found in the keys of F and C, and so can be used as a pivot chord in a modulation from F to the dominant.

Pizzicato (abbreviated to pizz.). A direction to pluck, instead of bow, string(s) on a violin, viola, cello or double bass. Cancelled by the direction 'arco' – with the bow.

Plagal cadence. A cadence ending with the tonic chord (I), preceded by the subdominant (IV). Appropriate where a restful finality is required, it is used sparingly in tonal music.

Quartal harmony. Harmony based on the interval of a 4th (e.g. with chords such as A–D–G), rather than on the interval of a 3rd as in triads and 7th chords.

Ragtime. A style of popular music that emerged in the 1890s and continued throughout the first two decades of the 20th century. It is usually in $\frac{2}{4}$ time and is characterised by a syncopated melody played against a march-like accompaniment.

Range. The interval between the lowest note in a passage and the highest (for example, a melody with middle C as the lowest note and C in the third space of the treble stave as the highest note has a range of an octave).

Recitative. A piece for solo voice in an opera, cantata or oratorio (often before an **aria**) in which clear projection of words is the main concern. In many recitatives the music is functional rather than of great interest in itself, with the accompaniment often just for continuo.

Relative major and minor. Keys that have the same key signature but a different scale (e.g. F major and D minor, both with a key signature of one flat). A relative minor is three semitones lower than its relative major (e.g. the tonic of D minor is three semitones lower than the tonic of its relative major, F major).

Riff. A short, catchy melodic figure, repeated like an **ostinato** and commonly found in rock, pop and jazz.

Ripieno. The players other than the soloists in a Baroque concerto grosso. (Italian for 'filling up' or 'completion'.)

Ritornello form. A structure used in Baroque music in which an opening instrumental section (called the ritornello) introduces the main musical ideas. This returns, often in shortened versions and in related keys, between passages for one or more soloists. The complete ritornello (or a substantial part of it) returns in the tonic key at the end.

Rondo. A piece in which an opening section in the tonic key is heard several times, with different material ('episodes'), usually in different keys, between these repetitions. The simplest rondo shape is A B A C A (where A is the recurring section and B and C are episodes), but this can be extended, for instance with additional episode(s) and further repeats of the A section.

Scherzo. A fast movement which, from the early 19th century, usually replaced the minuet in a symphony or sonata. It is generally similar in structure to a minuet (with a contrasting trio), and usually in simple triple time; but there are several examples in duple time by later Romantic composers, for example the Brahms scherzo in *NAM* (no. 18, page 231) which alternates between compound duple ($\frac{6}{8}$) and simple duple ($\frac{2}{4}$).

Scotch snap. *See* **Lombardic rhythm.**

Sequence. Immediate repetition of a melodic or harmonic idea at a different pitch.

Serial. In serial music all (or most) pitches are derived from an underlying fixed series of pitches that can be manipulated by transposition, inversion and retrograding (being played backwards). A widely practiced form of serialism in the mid 20th century used a series (or 'row') of twelve notes that included every note of the chromatic scale once.

Siciliana. A type of instrumental or vocal movement popular in the 17th and 18th centuries, often used to suggest pastoral scenes. Normally fairly slow and in compound time ($\frac{6}{8}$ or $\frac{12}{8}$).

Simple time. A metre in which the main beat is sub-divided into two equal portions. Opposite of **compound time.**

Singspiel. An opera with German words, some of which are spoken not sung. Most singspiels are from the late 18th and early 19th centuries, and the comic element is often strong. ('Singspiel' is German for 'sung play'.) *See also* **Opera.**

Sonata. An instrumental work, commonly in three or four movements. From the late Baroque period onwards, sonatas are usually for solo keyboard or for single melody instrument and keyboard. 'Trio sonatas' (middle to late Baroque) are normally for two violins and continuo.

Sonata form. A form developed in the Classical period from binary form. The first section is the exposition, beginning in the tonic and ending in a closely-related key, often with two contrasting groups of melodic material (first subject, second subject). The second section commonly includes a development section, followed by a recapitulation with first and second subjects restated in the tonic. Sonata form is used generally for the first quick movement from a Classical or post-Classical symphony or sonata, and sometimes also for other movements.

Stride. A jazz piano style partly derived from ragtime, in particular from the characteristic left-hand pattern which repeatedly 'strides' from a low note or chord on a strong beat to a higher chord on a weak beat. Stride piano was particularly popular in the 1920s.

Substitution chord. A chord, especially in jazz, used to replace one of the chords in a harmonic progression. It has a similar harmonic function to the chord it replaces, and may have one or more notes in common with it. For example, in Ellington's *Black and Tan Fantasy* (*NAM* 49), the B♭ major 12-bar blues (bars 29–40) has a Cm⁷ chord (C–E♭–G–B♭) in bar 37 in place of the expected E♭ chord (E♭–G–B♭).

Suspension. A suspension occurs at a change of chord, when one part hangs on to (or repeats) a note from the old chord, creating a dissonance, after which the delayed part resolves by step (usually down) to a note of the new chord.

Sustaining pedal. The right pedal on a piano that, while held down, sustains note(s) even after the fingers have been lifted from the keys.

Swing. A popular big-band style mainly of the 1930s. 'Swung rhythms' typically feature pairs of quavers in which the first is lengthened in performance, the second shortened.

Symphony. A work for orchestra with several (usually three or four) movements in different tempi – in effect a sonata for orchestra rather than for one or a few instruments.

Syncopation. The shifting of stress from a strong to a weak beat. For example, in a $\frac{4}{4}$ bar with the rhythm ♩ ♩ ♩, the minim (a relatively long note beginning on a weak beat) is syncopated.

Ternary form. A musical structure of three sections in which the outer sections are similar and the central one contrasting (ABA).

Texture. The relationship between the various simultaneous lines in a passage of music, dependent on such features as the number and function of the parts and the spacing between them.

Tierce de Picardie. A major 3rd in the final tonic chord of a passage in a minor key.

Tonality. The system of major and minor keys in which one note (the tonic, or key note) has particular importance, and in which various keys are related. Especially in the 18th and 19th centuries, tonality is established by the use of functional harmony. For exam purposes, questions on tonality might also include indentifying music that is modal (based on one or more modes) or that is based on non-western scales. Western music that uses neither keys nor modes is described as atonal (without tonality).

Tremolo. A rapid and continuous repetition of a single note or two alternating notes.

Trill. An ornament in which two adjacent notes rapidly and repeatedly alternate (the note bearing the trill sign and the one above it). The symbol for a trill is *tr*.

Triplet. A group of three equal notes played in the time normally taken by two notes of the same type. For example, a triplet of quavers is played in the time taken by two normal quavers.

Tutti. Used in orchestral scores to show that everyone is required to play, not just soloist(s) or other reduced forces. (Italian for 'all'.)

Twelve-bar blues. A standard chord sequence lasting 12 bars, used in the blues and other popular music. It is based on the tonic (I), subdominant (IV) and dominant (V) chords of a key. A common form is I–I–I–I, IV–IV–I–I, V–IV–I–I.

Una corda. The left pedal on a piano, which has a muting effect produced usually by shifting the action so that the hammers strike only one string where there is a group of two or three strings for a note (or strike off-centre where there is only one string).

Unison. Simultaneous performance of the same note or melody by two or more players or singers.

Verse anthem. *See* **Anthem**. In a verse anthem sections for soloist(s) alternate with those for the full choir.

Violino piccolo. In Baroque times, a type of small violin tuned higher than an ordinary violin (by a 3rd or a 4th), thus making it easier to play high notes. (Italian for 'small violin'.)

Vocalisation. A style of singing in which pitches are produced without distinct words. The term often refers to technical exercises for singers that focus on vowels, but composers have written textless vocal pieces for performance.

Whole-tone scale. A scale in which the interval between every successive note is a whole tone.